THE

Handbook
of Jewish
Meditation
Practices

Other Books and Tapes by Rabbi David A. Cooper

Books

God Is a Verb:
Kabbalah and the Practice of Mystical Judaism

A Heart of Stillness:
A Complete Guide to Learning the Art of Meditation

Silence, Simplicity & Solitude:
A Complete Guide to Spiritual Retreat at Home

Three Gates to Meditation Practice:
A Personal Journey into Sufism, Buddhism, and Judaism

Audiotapes

The Holy Chariot

Kabbalah Meditation

The Mystical Kabbalah

THE

Handbook
of Jewish
Meditation
Practices

A Guide for Enriching
the Sabbath and Other
Days of Your Life

RABBI DAVID A. COOPER

For People of All Faiths, All Backgrounds
JEWISH LIGHTS Publishing
Woodstock, Vermont

The Handbook of Jewish Meditation Practices:
A Guide to Enriching the Sabbath and Other Days of Your Life

Library of Congress Cataloging-in-Publication Data
Cooper, David A., 1939–
The handbook of Jewish meditation practices : a guide for enriching the Sabbath and other days of your life / David A. Cooper.
    p. cm.
Includes bibliographical references (p.).
ISBN 1-58023-102-0 (paperback)
1. Meditation—Judaism. 2. Spiritual life—Judaism. 3. Prayer—Judaism. 4. Jewish meditations. 5. Cabala. I. Title.
BM723 .C665 2000
296.7'2—dc21
                                                    00-011089

10 9 8 7 6 5 4 3 2 1

Manufactured in the United States
Cover design by Graciela Galup

Published by Jewish Lights Publishing
A Division of LongHill Partners, Inc.
Sunset Farm Offices, Rte. 4, P.O. Box 237
Woodstock, VT 05091
Tel: (802) 457 4000   Fax: (802) 457-4004
www.jewishlights.com

Contents

III. Kabbalistic Meditations   117

Appendixes

Introduction

> *You shall meditate on the Torah day and night, that you*
> *may hold firmly all [the wisdom teachings] written within*
> *it, and then you will thrive from all your actions and*
> *thoughts.*
>
> Joshua 1:8

The Handbook of Jewish Meditation Practices offers readers
background information on a variety of meditative techniques and suggests specific practices that can result in
invaluable "hands on" experience of what happens in the
mind and body when we alter our consciousness. This book,
originally titled *Renewing Your Soul*, has been revised and
amended to more comprehensively represent the growing
body of knowledge and practice that falls into the category of
Jewish meditation.

As a student of meditation techniques in a wide variety
of spiritual disciplines—including, in addition to Judaism,
Theravada Buddhism, Zen, Vajrayana, Hinduism, and
Sufism—I have found that many meditative practices are
common in all traditions, despite the fact that each tradition
clearly has its own style and methodology. Thus, a fair
amount of meditation is generic. For example, sitting in
silence is a universal practice, as is chanting repetitive
phrases, one-pointed concentration, being mindful of the
present moment, and taking time each day for reflection

(a practice many call prayer). These are all found in most traditions—only the language changes in how each practice is described.

There are, of course, many meditative practices unique to individual traditions. Zen has a great deal of *karma yoga*, which is a practice associated with mundane, everyday activities. Zen also has more exotic techniques expressed through highly ritualized forms such as archery and tea ceremony. Theravada Buddhism tends to be abstemious, extremely basic, with simple robes and begging bowls, no meals after lunch, and extended periods of silent practice that last weeks or months at a time. On the other hand, Vajrayana Buddhism is complicated, intellectual, colorful, and filled with imagery. Hinduism has a colorful side that is highly devotional, with many deities and much singing, dancing, and feasting. It also has a more austere side, with a number of forms of yoga that defy scientific explanation. Sufism is built on traditional Islamic practices of ablutions, prayer five times a day, and fasting during the month of Ramadan, with additional meditative expressions that include repetitive chanting of names of God for hours at a time, frequently accompanied by ecstatic whirling.

As there are many different forms of meditative practice, we must first define what we mean when we are discussing meditation. The "goal" of meditative practice in all spiritual endeavors is to experience our true nature. Each tradition has its own language for what this means. Libraries are filled with books discussing the similarities and differences of spiritual practice, but we can sum it up simply by saying that human consciousness seeks to know the truth of its own existence, its source, and its reason for being—if indeed there is any ultimate truth.

The word "goal" above is put in quotation marks to acknowledge that quite a few spiritual disciplines are adamant that having any goal or making any effort toward self-realization is, by definition, self-defeating. There are two sides to this argument. Some assert that just as an eye cannot see itself, except as a separate image, consciousness cannot be conscious of itself. The other argument is that all effort for self-realization is foolish as there is nothing to achieve; we intrinsically already have everything we need to know. As there is nothing to get, the very idea of a goal is deluded thinking.

This is a clear example of how language, the tool of rationality, is often inherently in conflict with mystical teaching. Meditative techniques are designed to help spiritual "aspirants" achieve altered states of consciousness. When this in fact occurs, the results often transcend rational explanation. Throughout history, mystics have been unable to directly communicate their experiences. Rather, they have found ways to transmit experiences indirectly through metaphor, poetry, or enigmatic wisdom teachings. Each mystical teacher finds his or her expression through the cultural structure in which he or she lives, with the culture's beliefs, values, attitudes, and opinions, all of which are molded by the era, surrounding communities, and general historical perspective in those times.

The teachings of these mystics, although not particularly rational, have profoundly influenced the history of humankind. They have birthed many spiritual traditions and have caused these traditions to branch into various directions. The mystics give us pause to reflect on the possibility of something more than life as we see it in front of us. They inspire us to seek more deeply, beyond appearances. In many ways, although from widely diverse backgrounds and even though they use their own distinctive languages, they speak about a common theme.

The metaphor for this is that whereas there are many paths up the mountain, there is only a single peak, higher than all others. Obviously, each person on the spiritual journey has his or her own natural dispositions and characteristics. Different paths up the mountain will be more readily accessible to some than others. For some, a path will seem to be a dead end; for others, the barriers they encounter are simply obstacles that need to be surmounted to get higher up the mountain. The mysteries of these spiritual paths defy explanation, and many spiritual adventurers spend their lives exploring a path and its divergent tracks with remarkable patience. In the end, however, no matter what path we take, the highest peak of truth remains the same for all who seek it.

Judaism is an extraordinary path for spiritual growth, as we shall see. It is a rich tradition with a long history. It is not really one path up the mountain, but many trails that occasionally are parallel but often go on totally different routes. With limited perspective, one might think that the result is that these paths will never meet again. But, when standing back, we can still see that there is only one highest peak and all paths ultimately lead to the One.

Often, people ask, "If they all lead to an ultimate truth, how do we choose our path?" This question raises many issues. It suggests that we have total free choice, but this is not completely true. We are constrained in many ways. We have our parentage, our character, our physical, emotional, and intellectual makeup, our society, our culture, our ancestry, our language, and so forth. All of these set parameters and incline us one way or another.

Clearly, Eastern spiritual and meditative traditions during the past century have become more accessible in the West. In absorbing some of these teachings, the West has modified, redefined, and remolded the practices to fit a more Western model. This simply is the way it works. So whatever path we "choose," we will adapt it to meet our needs.

As Eastern teachings, particularly in the arena of meditation, have grown in popularity, an interesting phenomenon has developed in the past twenty years. Under the influence of strong meditative practices, Westerners have increasingly been returning to their root traditions. When one is immersed in altered consciousness, it overflows into everyday life. Seen through these eyes, we discover that many elements of our lives and many aspects of our root traditions are meditation practices in and of themselves. It is out of this phenomenon that an entire new appreciation for the potential of Jewish meditation has dramatically evolved over the past decade.

While Jewish meditation as an identifiable collection of teachings is a relatively new phenomenon, meditative practices have been deeply rooted in Judaism for thousands of years. The essence of meditation is an integral part of traditional Jewish daily life, ritual, prayer, study of Torah, Talmud, and celebration of the Sabbath and the holy days. Indeed, meditation techniques are so fully integrated into traditional Jewish life that they were never separated out as unique practices of themselves. Today, many practitioners of traditional Judaism are highly skilled meditators in one way or another but they don't give this a name.

While very few Jewish teachers over the past two thousand years emphasized meditative techniques, per se, they often described how one can achieve higher states of consciousness through prayer or continuous study. We must keep in mind that until only the last couple of centuries, traditional Jewish life assumed certain daily activities had the potential for regular periods of self-reflection and contemplation. It was a given that people would have periods of quiet, that the Sabbath would be a day of rest, that time for prayer would be made each day, that one would pay close attention to food preparation, that, indeed, every facet of one's life would be under close scrutiny. The ideal was to live impeccably. This was what life was about. This impeccability by its nature requires experiencing many opportunities for meditative awareness in the context of expanded consciousness.

The most distinctive transformation Judaism has undergone in the past couple of hundred years is the way in which modern Jews live their daily lives. It is not surprising that the farther away we get from a traditional life style, the less meaningful we find the elements of Jewish practice. Each part loses something when separated from the whole. The complaint of a large number of people who want to be connected with their Judaism is that individual practices, like prayer or occasional Torah study, a Sabbath morning in a synagogue, or the celebration of a ritual, are primarily devoted to a form but lack a spiritual content.

On the other hand, many who have been discontented with Judaism have been drawn to simple practices of sitting quietly, chanting a few words in repetition, or singing to God while focused on basic thoughts of lovingkindness, forgiveness, gratitude, generosity, and so forth. The plain truth of the matter, of course, is that all these basic practices are within the repertoire of Judaism, but are often hidden, obscured by layers of a tradition originally designed for another way of life. The reason Jewish-oriented meditation has become popular so quickly is that it provides a foundation in a subtle but profound way upon which these individual practices can link with the heart of the tradition. In this way, there is a new opportunity for modern practitioners to access a deep spirituality through elements of Judaism that are bonded in some way with an inner pulse that has continued over the centuries, and will continue for centuries to come.

The roots of Jewish meditation have often been hidden in the oral tradition passed directly from teacher to student, or in kabbalistic writings that are difficult to decipher. However, many Jewish meditative techniques have been common knowledge and were widely practiced in various ways over the centuries. There are many different Hebrew words for these techniques.

For example, the word *hitbonenut* usually refers to a type of contemplation in which one focuses one's thought on a subject that has an intrinsic potential to alter one's consciousness. Another word used in a similar context is *histakkelut*, which is a type of contemplation that involves visualizations. *Hitbodedut*, often used to describe meditation, means to seclude oneself physically, to separate oneself. The term *kavannah*, which means intention, is also used to describe a meditative, focused state of mind. The term *hishtavut,* meaning equanimity, is viewed as foundation for attaining higher states of awareness. The idea of *bittul ha-yesh,* literally to nullify the sense of "is-ness," is descriptive of letting go of one's self-awareness, also viewed as an essential element of expanded consciousness. So, too, the term *meserit ha-nefesh,* sacrifice of the vital soul, is a way of referring to the state of selflessness.

Aryeh Kaplan, the most prolific modern writer to discuss the Jewish contemplative approach, lists several types of Jewish meditation in his books *Jewish Meditation* and *Meditation and the Bible.* One is called *suach,* a state of prayerful elevation in which the meditator communes with the divine Source of Life. Another is called *hagah,* or *higayon,* in which the meditator uses repetition—much like a mantra—to enter a state of altered consciousness. A third method, *ranan,* involves drenching the emotions until the meditator attains a level of ecstasy. In the East this is referred to as *bhakti,* in which one attains a connection with the Divine through concentrated devotional practice.

Yet another method of Jewish meditation is called *shasha.* It is one of the higher and more difficult forms in that the meditator is continuously pressing the limits of the mind. It is as if there were a sphere of light—called *awareness*—that seems always out of reach. The meditator dances on the periphery, not quite absorbed in the sphere and yet not really outside it. On this edge of awareness, one attains a deep state of rapture. At a higher level, however, one comes to the ultimate realization that there never was an edge in the first place, and one transcends rapture into yet a more inclusive state. This is the state of *devekut,* being at one with all.

Meditation and the Talmud

Judaism has a long history of contemplative and meditative practice. A well-known reference to the mystical side of Judaism is recorded in the Talmud (*Berachot* 32b) in a discussion about prayer. It says that the first *hasidim,* ancient pious practitioners, meditated an hour before prayer and an hour after. Because the Talmud itself is an old document, the ancient ones to whom it refers must have lived well over two thousand years ago.

The Talmud notes that if these practitioners did the required three prayers a day lasting an hour each, they would have spent nine hours a day in meditation and prayer. It then inquires, in typically talmudic fashion: If these people spent nine hours a day in contemplative activity, how could they keep up their studies of Torah, and, moreover, how could they earn a living? The answer it provides is that these contemplatives did not have any difficulty in learning because they never forgot anything, and they did not have to work so hard because, for them, a little effort went a long way. The important point here is that the Talmud gives clear support to the contemplative life style, and it suggests that a strong commitment to inner work will be rewarded in mysterious ways.

In another section (*Hagigah* 11b), the Talmud gives detailed instructions about teaching the secrets of Judaism's hidden mysteries. For example, there was a profound and esoteric teaching called the mystery of "descent into the Chariot." The mystical Chariot was the means by which one could use contemplative techniques to be transported to higher realms of awareness. In this section of the Talmud, it is written that a teacher was not permitted to discuss anything regarding the Chariot unless the student was already accomplished on the highest level. Today we might call this "postdoctorate" spiritual education.

Throughout this same talmudic section, the great masters are reluctant to answer their students' questions regarding the mystical underpinning of the creation. Indeed, the Talmud discusses at great length the dangers of esoteric exploration. It is here that the famous story is told about four sages who entered the *pardes*—the orchard or garden of mystical awareness. Three of the four were not well prepared for the shock of experiencing the overwhelming light of expanded consciousness. One died as soon as he looked around him, another instantly went mad, and a third became a disbeliever. Only one, Rabbi Akiva, came out unharmed. As Rabbi Akiva is one of the most important figures in the Talmud, it is of great significance that his mystical and contemplative character is a point of considerable distinction. Clearly, the talmudic scholars had extraordinary respect for contemplative practice.

The Sabbath

The most important feature of contemplative Judaism is the celebration of the weekly Sabbath, called Shabbat* in Hebrew. Shabbat is a day of *menucha*, a time of spiritual renewal. According to the sages, spiritual renewal can be accomplished when we are able to separate ourselves from mundane activity and thought.

Shabbat is often misunderstood as simply a day of rest, but it has much deeper implications. For example, we often rest by lying on the couch watching television, by going to a ball game, or by taking a vacation. But the type of rest that leads to spiritual renewal is different. Menucha requires quieting the mind and soul through spiritual practice, dwelling on the higher realms, absorbing oneself in contemplation of the Divine. From this we gain a new appreciation of our relationship with the universe and hopefully deepen our awareness and our sense of purpose.

The Sabbath is so important in Judaism, it is one of the Ten Commandments (*Remember the Sabbath, to keep it holy*). There is more Jewish law regarding Shabbat than just about any other subject. Indeed, the laws pertaining to Shabbat are the foundation for observance of the major Jewish holy days throughout the year, and all Jewish commentators agree that even though it appears every week, Shabbat is the most important day in the Jewish calendar.

---

*Throughout this book, Sabbath and Shabbat are used interchangeably.

The exercises outlined in this guide utilize methods that can achieve some of the meditative states described above. Although most of the meditative exercises in this guide are related to Judaism, the reader does not have to be Jewish to gain the benefits. Just as many of us have acquired significant insight through Eastern meditation, in the same way, the exercises outlined in this book can be used effectively by people from all walks of life.

Obviously, extensive practice is required to attain deep meditative skills; this is not something that we aspire to in only a few days. The objective of this book is to describe different approaches so that busy people can begin to appreciate the benefits of contemplative technique. This experience, it is hoped, will open new passageways of wisdom that can be pursued over the years to come. In any case, following any of the schedule of practices outlined in this book will almost certainly lead the reader into a quieter and more insightful state of mind.

The first section of this book describes a dozen basic Jewish meditation practices. Many of the meditations described in this first section are prerequisites for practices that appear later in the book. This particularly applies to sitting practice, walking meditation, psycho-spiritual journaling, kavannah and continuity practice, and prayer. All of these are basic foundation practices upon which others are built. The reader will quickly discover that simply reading about these meditation methods does not accomplish much. The meditations must be experienced to be fully appreciated. Moreover, it is far more beneficial to spend a few days repeating one practice over and over again than to skim over a dozen mediations without experiencing any in depth.

The second section, Jewish Retreats, describes in a segment called Solo Retreats, how a practitioner can begin to master meditation by regularly spending a full day on retreat. Readers are invited to take Sabbath days to experience the power of nonstop repetitive practice. All of the methods described in the first section of the book on basic practice can be used individually or in combination to have a strong retreat experience.

This second section of the book also includes a segment called Family Retreats. This part describes a basic, gentle way to introduce a contemplative approach to Shabbat for families (or interested individuals). It suggests ways to use the basic ritual of Shabbat in a meditative fashion that adds simple joy to the weekly experience, and brings us closer in relationship to each other.

Finally, the last section of the book, Kabbalistic Meditations, offers over a dozen techniques of chanting and visualizations that can engender transformative experiences. These visualizations are best done when meditators have experience with the basic methods of sitting and quieting the mind, as described early in the book. However, these practices can be powerful experiences as well for those who have not had prior meditative training.

Use this book as a guide. Skip around if you wish, but be sure to do the meditations. Don't simply read about them. Take at least the minimum time suggested for each and experience it—not just once, but a number of times. You will find that each time the experience is different. Only in this way will you benefit from the potential meditation practice.

Modern civilization suffers from a chronic condition of anemic, starving souls. The sages teach us that if we feed our souls, we will experience a new kind of happiness and more meaning in life. They say we will see nature more clearly, and a new world of inner peace will open. Renew the soul and one's perspective of daily life will completely change. It is simply a matter of taking time, slowing down, shifting mundane consciousness into realms of higher insight, and giving oneself the gift of reflection and contemplation.

Many books address the process of deepening our spiritual connections in theory, but do not discuss specific exercises to support this aspiration. This guide is designed for those who wish to actively participate in spiritual practice. Contemplative insight is acquired only through direct experience; it is not something that can be realized through only reading or study. Renew your soul. It is up to you. Be kind to yourself. As the Talmud teaches:

> "One who studies Torah for the purpose of teaching is [only] given the means to study and teach. However, one who studies in order to practice is [not only] given the means to study and teach, [but also] to observe and to practice [thereby having deeper understanding]."

Pirke Avot 4:6

Basic Jewish Meditation Practices

Isaac went out into the field to meditate at sundown, and he raised his eyes to see camels approaching. Rebecca [on a camel] raised her eyes and when she saw Isaac, she slid off her camel [for she knew he was somebody special]. She said [excitedly] to the servant, "Who is this man who walks in the field to meet us?" And the servant said, "It is my master [who sent me to find you to be his wife.]"

Genesis 24:63–65

Throughout history, human beings have found time to retreat from their daily lives in search of inner peace. Almost all profound thought in the history of human awareness has evolved through reflection, contemplation, and meditation.

These days we do not seem to have much time for contemplative exploration. Life is complicated and busy. Our minds are moving at supersonic speeds. Advertisers and the news media have learned that the only way to capture our attention is with rapid-fire, sensational, highly evocative material. Advances in technology—those wonderful inventions that were supposed to provide more leisure time—have overwhelmed our lives so that, ironically, there is hardly any time left to be with ourselves, ponder the mysteries of the universe, or gain a personal sense of purpose in life.

Everyone finds time to notice a beautiful sunrise, the autumn change of color, or the epiphanies that spring forth each time we experience something magical in nature. These are moments that touch our souls. Indeed, these are the times that seem to make life worthwhile. But, whereas we have learned to take occasional vacations to refresh and revitalize our bodies, how often do we take time to consciously renew our souls?

The need to attend the inner spirit was the primary thrust that initiated most of the world's religions. This need remains, ostensibly, at the heart of spiritual traditions. But Westerners are finding it increasingly difficult to nourish the soul in religious traditions developed many centuries ago. We may feel comfortable with the inherent truths of our spiritual heritage, but we usually find that the outward form of the tradition expressed by our grandparents fails to comfort our innermost place of longing.

This, I believe, is largely the result of our state of mind when we engage in spiritual practice. If the mind is extremely busy, racing from one thought to another, there is little opportunity to fully experience the deeper content of any spiritual experience. We need to focus our concentration if we wish to have the opportunity to appreciate the nuances of classical wisdom teachings.

When people are touched deeply by particularly insightful thoughts, they will often say that the experience expanded their awareness. But it is more accurate to say that deep insights are contingent upon first entering a state of altered consciousness by slowing down our normal mental processes.

My own experience, and the experience of dozens of people with whom I have worked, is that one always uncovers hidden gems when exploring traditional practices with a quiet mind. Many people complain about their overactive, busy thought processes, sometimes called "monkey mind," yet, in fact, it is relatively easy to achieve a more composed mind state. In just a short period of consistent meditative practice, we can begin to steady the mind and realize deeper levels of self-reflection. This is the beginning of true liberation.

For those who attend regular Friday night services, it is very difficult to work all day, rush home in crowded traffic, hurry to get to synagogue on time, and then throw some invisible inner switch in order to fully join in the spirit of welcoming the Sabbath. This does not work well for most people; their minds remain engaged in business, reflecting on the past or planning for the future even while sitting in services.

It is even more traumatic when major holy days arrive. For example, how is it possible to maintain a busy workday just before the arrival of Yom Kippur, hurry to hear the call of the *kol nidre* melody, and be fully absorbed in the holiest day of the Jewish calendar without the mind getting excited over the rise or fall of that day's stock market or some other mundane thought. This is asking a great deal of our nervous systems.

My appreciation of the depths of Judaism owes a great deal to receptive states of mind that I achieved through practices that established a strong sense of inner peace. I discovered in this meditative process that Judaism itself has a rich contemplative heritage. Frankly, this is not well known. Mainstream Judaism today does not emphasize the practice of quieting the mind. Indeed, Judaism is an intellectual, verbose, assertive tradition in which I have often heard it said, "Silence and meditation are not Jewish."

I believed this for many years. Thus, when a yearning for inner stillness began to quicken in my soul, Judaism did not seem to be a likely resource for contemplative engagement. However, once I investigated many other spiritual resources, and thereby gained the open and broad perspective of a meditative mind, I experienced Judaism as an enormously rich, contemplative tradition; indeed, I am continually discovering new gems hidden within.

The following are a dozen basic practices in the Jewish world. Many of these meditation techniques are found in other traditions as well. They have a Jewish flavor when practiced in a Jewish environment when they help us connect more deeply with our souls and give us greater insight into the meaning of our lives. Thus, whereas sitting quietly for 45 minutes is simply a generic meditation technique, sitting quietly for 45 minutes in shul specifically to prepare for Yom Kippur, to connect more deeply with the kol nidre, or to listen more intently to the sound of the shofar is a Jewish-oriented meditation. Moreover, while prayer is a widespread method in its general form, specifically the use of Hebrew and the writings of the Torah provide a Jewish container for prayer that distinctly affects the nature of the prayers.

Take your time with each of these practices. Notice how they slow you down. Allow yourself to become absorbed in the moment. We already have everything we need to be at peace. We simply need to quiet down to discover this truth for ourselves.

ABLUTIONS/MIKVEH (30–60 minutes)

> No person, even if completely clean, could enter the Temple Court without immersing [in a *mikveh*]. The high priest underwent five immersions and ten sanctifications on the day of Yom Kippur.
>
> Babylonian Talmud: *Yoma* 30a

O ne of the oldest known spiritual practices is to symbolically bathe and cleanse our bodies— not to rid ourselves of physical impurities, but to attain spiritual purification.

A common practice in traditional Judaism is to spiritually purify through immersion in a *mikveh*, which is any gathering of "living water" in which one can submerge completely. As long as there is enough water to completely engulf the body, any natural gathering of water—rivers, ponds, lakes, streams, even the ocean—can be used for spiritual purification.

Water gatherings that are not part of nature qualify as mikvehs only if they meet rabbinic criteria. Water separated from the earth and placed in a vessel, such as a pipe used in normal plumbing, is no longer considered "living water." Therefore, technically, a regular bathtub or swimming pool does not qualify as a mikveh.

Nonetheless, the primary principle of spiritual purification is based upon our intentions. The famous twelfth-century Jewish philosopher Maimonides said, "One who has the intention in one's own heart to purify the soul from the defilement of wrongful thoughts and false beliefs…will bring his/her soul into the waters of perfect knowing, as it says: 'And I will sprinkle upon you pure water, and purify you from all your uncleanliness'" (Mishna Torah, *Mikveot* 11:12).

If you happen to be near a body of "living water" or near an established mikveh, a wonderful way to begin the day is with an immersion. Many traditional Jewish men go to the mikveh daily to cleanse themselves and to prepare for morning prayers. A large percentage attend the mikveh the day before the Sabbath or the day before the holy days that occur throughout the year.

Traditional Jewish women always use the mikveh at the time of month when Jewish law requires spiritual purification in preparation for the act of procreation. Thus, use of the mikveh is a major spiritual practice in traditional Judaism. In any case, if you have the ability to use a "kosher" mikveh, please take your time in the process and try to develop deep inner awareness. (Cultivating inner awareness—*kavannah*, or intention—is discussed later.)

Even if you are unable to use an official mikveh that meets all rabbinic requirements, you may still engage in the practice of doing spiritual ablutions with water that comes directly out of the tap. Here is one way of experiencing this purifying practice:

1. One of our first acts in the morning normally is to relieve our bladders. Right after this, using a cup or glass, pour water over your right hand from the wrist down, then over your left hand from the wrist down. While pouring the water, imagine that any negative energy that may be lingering from this night's sleep—perhaps a heavy dream or an otherwise agitated night—is passing out of your fingertips and down the drain. Repeat this three times. This is our first act of purification of the day. It should be noted that traditional Jews do this every day of their lives.

2. Now, with only a wet washcloth (no soap), taking your time and frequently rinsing the cloth, wash your forehead and then dry it. It may be useful for you to be seated while doing these purifications, either on a chair or on the floor, using a bowl as your source of water. Wash your eyes and then dry them. Follow the same procedure with your nose, ears, mouth, cheeks, jaw, and neck. In each

area, as you are washing it or drying it, let your imagination carry you anywhere it will, and allow yourself to create affirmations that are spiritually oriented, using ideas such as the following:

"I am cleansing my forehead, and all that it represents, so that I can be free from critical and judgmental thoughts, whether they are thoughts about myself or about others.

"I am cleansing my eyes so that I will be able to see things as they really are in order to develop deep compassion for life.

"I am cleansing my nose so that I will be able to smell the fragrance of mystical delight and can dwell in the beauty of nature.

"I am cleansing my ears so that I will be able to hear the deeper truths of all that I encounter, and not be corrupted by gossip and unskillful speech.

"I am purifying around my mouth so that I can be more aware of the words that I speak, and will be careful not to cause harm by speaking unskillfully.

"I am cleansing my cheeks so that I will be able to smile with radiance and appreciate all the gifts that I have been given.

"I am cleansing my jaw so that I will be able to relax and be present at all times.

"I am washing my neck so that I will be flexible and able to understand the viewpoints of others."

These quotes are only suggestions to help acclimate you to the process. Once you are flowing freely with your own thoughts and imagination, allow yourself to reach deeply within so that you can pull forth your most profound affirmations.

3. When you have completed ablutions from the neck upward, continue with the rest of the body, working your way down: shoulders, upper arms, lower arms, hands, each finger, upper back, lower back, upper chest, breasts, center chest, abdomen, genital area, thighs, knees, calves, ankles, and feet, including each toe—all the while being sure with every part of the body to find an affirmation.

Some people find themselves crying when engaged in the process of ablutions. The water outside raises the tears within. Feel free to burst if this is what you need at this time. The idea here is to begin the process of spiritual purification, whatever it takes. Moreover, if you find that you need more than an hour for this practice, by all means take more time.

This marvelous practice can be used each morning, no matter how much time you give it. It is exceptionally useful the first morning of a retreat, to set the tone for the first day (see retreats described later). Notice that the process is simply with plain water and a washcloth; it is not supposed to take the place of normal bathing, in which scrubbing with soap is the norm. Soap is for cleaning the body, whereas this process is for freeing the soul.

SITTING PRACTICE (30–60 minutes)

> The ancient pious ones used to meditate for an
> hour before prayer to build concentration on the
> heavenly realms. Even if greeted by a king, they
> did not answer him; even if a snake encircled
> their feet, they did not break their concentration.
>
> Babylonian Talmud: *Berachot* 30b

E very tradition has spiritual practices to quiet the
mind by some form of meditative technique.
The most basic of these techniques is to learn how to sit still
and do nothing. Although sitting still may sound quite
simple, it is a challenging experience for even the most
skilled meditator.

Learning how to sit still deepens our willpower and
concentration. As we become more accomplished, we gain
insight into the workings of our minds. This experience in
itself is so powerful that a large number of traditions focus
entirely on refining the ability to sit meditatively.

Many people erroneously equate the discipline of sitting
still with Eastern practitioners. Indeed, Westerners who first
experience profound states of awareness through quieting the
mind often associate this altered consciousness with
Buddhism, Taoism, Hinduism, or some other Eastern spiritual
tradition. But attaining deepened awareness by meditative
sitting is a universal practice, common in Western as well as
Eastern traditions, and is readily found in Christianity, Islam,
and Judaism.

Here are instructions for becoming accomplished in the
fundamental practice of sitting still.

Sit Comfortably

Find a comfortable place on the floor or on a chair so
that you can sit with your back held fairly straight. This is
usually accomplished by placing a cushion or pillow beneath

the buttocks. It is better not to lean against a wall or a chair, which may increase your tendency to slump or to become drowsy.

Do Not Move When Meditating

If sitting in a chair, place a cushion under your feet. If seated on the floor, cross your legs in a comfortable way, using padding if necessary under your knees or ankles. Your hands can be placed in any position, resting on your thighs or knees or in your lap, as long as the shoulders remain relaxed. The idea is to be positioned comfortably, relatively straight, so that you are able to sit for the entire period of this meditation *without voluntarily moving at all.* (Of course, there are always subtle movements connected with one's breathing.)

Do Not Look at the Time

When meditating alone, you will need a beeper-timer—available in many inexpensive watches. Although beginning meditators usually sit for about 30 minutes, you will discover that a more complete experience can be gained at 45 minutes. There is no need to sit any longer than this, but some experienced meditators prefer 1-hour periods. In any case, set your timer when you begin your sit and *do not look at the time until you hear the beep.*

Focus Attention on the Breath

Although a primary meditative discipline is to sit very still, the torso will continue to expand and contract around each breath. Bring your awareness to these involuntary body movements, trying all along not to control the breath but to breathe normally.

This is where we begin to build concentration. The idea is to notice the body movements of every single breath. You may wish to focus on the stomach or the chest as it rises and falls with the breath, or on the total body experience from the tip of the nostrils to the base of the abdomen.

The key to building concentration is to bring interest into the practice. Try to be aware of all the different qualities of each breath, and how each differs from every other. Try to be aware precisely when each expansion begins and ends, precisely when each contraction begins and ends, and what happens in between.

Notice the Mind

When you are completely aware of the detailed body movements around the breath, you are present in the moment. You will soon realize, however, that the mind will continuously capture your attention and carry you away into thought. The thinking process often blankets our awareness of the breath. As soon as you notice that you are thinking, quickly and gently—*without self-criticism or recriminations*—bring your awareness back to the body movement around the breath. You will do this over and over and over again, dozens or hundreds of times in every sitting meditation. This constant call on one's attention to stay with the experience of the breath is the crucial meditative act that slowly but surely quiets the mind and leads to profound insights.

Stay with the Practice

Habituated to perpetual activity, our minds do not easily accept the bridle of constant awareness. The more we assert control by focusing our attention on a primary object of observation—such as the breath—the more the mind will try to divert our concentration. It has an amazing arsenal and is extraordinarily devious in the tactics that it uses. Some of its most powerful weapons are doubt, anger, frustration, desire, aversion, sleepiness, boredom, despair, concern, jealousy, and, of course, the two biggest: pain and fear.*

---

*See my book *A Heart of Stillness* (SkyLight Paths, 1999) for detailed descriptions of how to work with various mind states while meditating.

Although the meditation practice is simply to sit quietly observing the experience of the breath rising and falling, we come under the attack of our own minds trying to take back control. This is a battle that all meditators experience. Sometimes the mind wins and we move our arms, legs, head, or neck, or we terminate our practice before the period is up. But as long as we come back again to the meditative posture and awareness of the breath, sooner or later we gain the upper hand. It is then that we experience enormous insight into the workings of our minds and achieve a profound sense of liberation. However, if in the early stages of meditation we allow the mind to convince us to quit altogether, to let go of our practice in building awareness, we never learn the truth that *we are not our minds.*

LONG-TERM BENEFITS OF QUIETING THE MIND

The baseline practice of sitting still and doing nothing can be used as your primary meditation practice. Some people prefer doing this to all other meditative techniques. The deeper we go into the experience of slowing down our busy minds, the more sensitive and aware we become of our surroundings. We begin to see hidden gems in everything we observe, and we discover new levels of appreciation in our daily lives. When we achieve more refined levels of awareness through quieting the mind, the result is an ever-deep-ening spiritual consciousness that opens the heart and renews the soul.

Meditative sitting is the baseline practice of most spiritual retreats. While on retreat, sitting is usually done a number of times each day at the very least. On some retreats, the entire schedule is focused on silent sitting and walking practice, often including an accumulation of 8 hours or more of sitting each day of the retreat. This can be an extraordinarily powerful experience, especially when continued for many days in a row as we do on week-long Jewish meditation retreats.*

Please consider for yourself a daily experience of 30–60 minutes of sitting practice, following the advice mentioned above: Sit in a comfortable position, do not move, bring your awareness to the movement of the torso around the breath, try to bring interest to the variations of the breath, notice your thoughts, and gently, constantly come back to the experience of the breath. That's all you need to do for this practice, and you will discover that as simple as it sounds, it is exceedingly difficult to be quiet for very long without getting caught in the web of thought. After a while you can become proficient in this spiritual exercise, and then the calmness and balance you experience will deepen your understanding of why there are so many practitioners of sitting meditation.

It is why the Talmud teaches:

"All my life I have lived among wise teachers, yet I have found nothing better for oneself than silence. Rather than study, practice is the main teacher."

Pirke Avot 1:17

---

*For more information on Jewish meditation retreats, see the Appendix for resources.

MORNING BLESSINGS/GRATITUDE
(30–45 minutes)

> I will praise you because I am awesomely made.
> Marvelous is your Creation; my soul knows this well.
>
> Psalms 139:14

A considerable number of meditation exercises are related to the physical body, either in specific postures, or in ritual movements. Although physical exercises help us stretch and relax, when used as a form of meditation they can benefit us on deeper levels. Thus, rather than doing any physical exercises in a rote fashion with a wandering mind, it is much more productive to maintain awareness of our bodies and our minds as much as possible.

A number of moving exercises have been introduced into morning practices by people who are engaged in Rabbi Zalman Schachter-Shalomi's approach to Jewish renewal. One of these exercises uses the traditional morning blessings in the prayer service as a guide. Accompanying the words, the practitioner pantomimes them with body movements. Another exercise uses the Hebrew alphabet to describe postures that are like the *asanas* of hatha yoga. Still another uses the Hebrew alphabet as a basis for flowing movements that are similar to tai chi chuan. Finally, there is a walking meditation that incorporates the experience of body movement with the awareness of everything that is taking place around us. We will explore some of these methods in this book.

The standard morning blessings are contained in most *siddurim* (Jewish prayer books). If you are accustomed to using these traditional *brachot hashachar* (morning blessings), please do so. Listed below are nontraditional blessings that seem to be more personally relevant for many people.

You may wish to develop your own set of blessings. The idea is to have a list of acknowledgments and affirmations that you can say daily as a morning routine. Over time, this process of offering blessings warms the heart and opens pathways to the soul.

The movements described here are custom-designed. I provide them as a guide but do not intend to imply that this is the "right" way. You may wish to find another way to physically express your feelings. Do what comes naturally for you.

Here are nontraditional morning blessings:

1. "I am so thankful to be alive, to experience moment by moment the mystery of life. Thank you, infinite Source of Life, for keeping me alive."

> Standing, facing east—where the sun rises—let the tips of the fingers of both hands touch the sternum. Then lift the arms upward and make a big circle with the hands—encircling the world—until the hands once again rest on the breastplate.

2. "I am so thankful to have my body parts working in harmony with one another, keeping me healthy. Thank you, infinite Source of Life, for keeping me healthy."

> Standing, allow the fingers to brush over the eyes, ears, nose, and mouth. Let the hands move down the neck, down the torso. Squatting, allow the hands to move down the legs until they come to rest on the feet. Then, rising, sweep the hands upward, retracing over the body until at the head the hands move straight upward, stretching as high as possible. Stand on the tips of the toes, and then relax, dropping the arms to the sides of the body.

3. "I am thankful to have my mind working in balance so that I can distinguish between light and dark and can discriminate to find my path in life. Thank you, infinite Source of Life, for giving me a wonderful mind."

Standing or seated, close the ears with the thumbs. While holding the ears closed, place the index fingers over the eyes, close the nostrils with the third finger—allowing a slight amount of air to flow—and put the ring and little fingers over the mouth. When all are in position, the primary sensory organs are cut off. Then after a minute or two release this position, allowing the sensory input to flood in.

4. "I am thankful for my relationships with family, friends, and associates so that we can help one another in learning about loving, helping, caring, and being present for one another. Thank you, infinite Source of Life, for my family, friends, and associates."

Standing, hold the hands as if receiving a large ball. Pull the hands upward into the chest, and cross the hands over the heart. Then push the hands outward until they are fully stretched forward. Circle the hands until they are again in a receiving mode—as if receiving a large ball. Repeat this cycle while reflecting on the mental images of family members, friends, and associates.

5. "I am thankful to be nourished each day, to have food and sustenance for myself and my family. Thank you, infinite Source of Life, nourisher and sustainer of the universe."

Standing, then crouching, gently wave the hands near the ground as if brushing them across the tops of grass. Then stand up and sway from side to side with arms outstretched as if brushing the hands across the tops of chest-high wheat in a large field. Repeat this movement a number of times.

6. "I am thankful to be clothed each day in garments that protect me from the elements, and to be protected as

well from unseen dangers. Thank you, infinite Source of Life, who clothes and protects the vital light of creation."

Standing, imagine holding a large cloth in both hands. Wrap this imaginary cloth around the body and over the head until you feel completely enclosed, with the arms tightly clasping the body as if hugging oneself. Now imagine being enclosed in the protective embrace of the Divine.

7. "I am thankful for my daily shelter, a roof over my head, a dwelling in which I can sleep safely, and the conveniences that minimize the physical hardships of daily survival. Thank you, Source of Life, who provides shelter from the rain, warmth from the cold, and secure comfort for a place of rest."

Lying down with the back on the floor, arms spread, palms up, legs slightly apart and relaxed, imagine feeling the entire body sinking into the floor. Be totally relaxed and receptive. Spend a few minutes like this.

8. "I am thankful to be free to choose my life's path, to go where I wish, to speak my mind, and to live in peace. Thank you, Source of Life, essence of Awareness, and Fountain of Peace."

Walking slowly, notice your body movements; notice all the visual and aural stimuli; be completely present in the moment. (See the upcoming section on Lucid Strolling for more guidance on this practice.) End the series of morning blessings with an affirmation to try to stay awake and present as much as possible this day—in a continual state of thankfulness and a deep sense of inner peace.

WALKING MEDITATION (30–45 minutes)

> **Abaye [a talmudic sage] said: "A person should always be in awe [of creation], speak softly, soothe anger, and speak peacefully with neighbors, relatives, and everyone...."**
>
> Babylonian Talmud: *Berachot* 17a

Walking meditation is one of the most useful techniques in all of contemplative practice. Most of us are lost in thought when we walk from one place to another, oblivious of everything around us. Yet, whereas we usually must arrange a special time for a sitting meditation, walking is something we normally do many times throughout the day. Once we learn how to bring a contemplative aspect to our walking, the opportunities for daily meditation multiply dramatically.

In many ways the walking practice is similar to sitting meditation. The objective is to focus attention on the experience of the body. However, while the focus of sitting meditation is typically on the breathing—feeling the chest or stomach moving with the breath—the focus of walking meditation is primarily on what is happening in the body from the hips down when we are walking. And a great deal is happening!

When we practice walking meditation, it is usually preferable to select a fairly level place about fifteen or twenty feet in length. The idea is to experience the process of walking, but not to be going anywhere. When we think we are going somewhere, it is much more difficult to concentrate on being where we actually are, that is, here in the moment. When we have nowhere to go, then we can be fully engaged in the contemplative walking experience. So, pick a place for walking, and then please follow along:

1. Standing still, legs slightly apart, knees slightly bent, eyes open or closed, experience the feeling of tension and

muscle control in the legs. Notice the hips, knees, and ankles. Feel the experience of the contact between the bottom of the feet and the ground. (Some people like to do walking meditation barefoot. Just be sure your feet are protected, even if it means wearing socks and/or sandals or shoes.)

2. Allow yourself to lean slightly to the right, and then to the left. Come to the center, balanced between the right and left. Then do the same leaning slightly forward and slightly back. Come to the center, balanced between all four directions. Experience the constant subtle shifting necessary to maintain the upright balance.

3. Now, do not move but begin to think about taking only one step with your right foot. *Do not move at all!* Just have the intention to take a step with the right foot. Notice what the body wants to do.

4. You are about to move your right foot to take a step. Now, do move, but *move very slowly,* noticing what the body must do in order for the foot to step. You will see that the entire weight needs to shift to the left side before you are able to lift the right foot. Begin to lift the foot, but do not raise it off the ground.

5. Now, moving further into the step, allow the foot to lift off the ground. Notice the dramatic shift in balance for the short period you are standing on one foot. Then notice the experience of placing the right foot on the ground again in the first step.

6. Bring the right foot back again to the original position, not yet having taken a step, and stand quietly for a moment. Now, once again, very slowly, noticing as much as possible, let yourself lift, move, and place the right foot in one step. As you are in each position, make quiet mental notes, such as "raising," "floating," and "setting," as you notice each movement of the foot.

Try to be as precise as possible in your noticing, being aware of exactly when the leg and foot begin the "raising," exactly when the toes leave the ground and the "floating" begins, and exactly when the foot touches the ground once again and the "setting" begins.

7. Allow the right foot to finish the step before taking a step with the left foot. (Ordinarily, when we walk at a normal pace, the raising of one foot overlaps the setting of the other. In this "slow walking" method, we finish one complete step before beginning another.) Thus you will continue walking, noting quietly to yourself something like, "raising…floating…setting, raising…floating…setting."

8. The mental notes should not mask your awareness of the complexity of the movement. Try to notice the flexing and stretching of muscles and tendons in the thighs and calves, the articulation of the joints, the feel of the skin as clothes brush against it, the pressure on the bottom of the foot. You may also notice how the breath is connected with the walking, the balancing of the body, the muscle groups of the back as each step is taken. Then you may notice the sights and sounds that are occurring with each step, and that every movement has its unique quality.

9. In the beginning, walk quite slowly, trying to notice as much as possible. Then, when you wish, you can quicken the pace. But you will soon realize that the faster you move, the less able you are to observe the details of your body and your surroundings. Nonetheless, after considerable training, one can continue a walking meditation even on the most crowded street at the busiest time of day.

10. Try to remember your walking practice whenever you can. It is a continuity practice, giving people the opportunity to bring meditation consciousness more frequently into everyday life. Use the walking meditation whenever you are able to remember that every body movement can be done with awareness, or it can be done in

an automatic fashion in which we are not really present in the moment.

The more we use the walking meditation, the more we appreciate that we can notice every body movement with awareness, or we can simply be in a rote, automatic state of mind in which we are not really present in the moment. This is continuous training to heighten our potential for sharpening our kavannah, our intentionality, which is at the foundation of all Jewish meditation practice.

LUCID STROLLING (30–45 minutes)

> When Abram was ninety-nine years old, the Lord
> appeared and said "I am the Almighty God; walk
> with me and be perfect."
>
> Genesis 17:1

The common walking meditation just described is based on a technique of concentration in which we pay close attention to the experience of the body as we move, feeling the muscular and tactile sensations. It is an excellent meditative method for calming the mind. Another way to engage in a walking meditation is to switch our attention from the body to all the external stimuli we experience throughout the walking period. In this walking exercise, we become finely attuned to outer sensory stimuli, noticing the profusion of sights, sounds, and odors.

The idea is to notice each moment as much as possible without thinking about anything, trying not to conceptualize. This is a difficult assignment, for the stimuli that pour in tend to arouse thoughts and memories. Yet, while we are thinking, it is virtually impossible to be present in the experience of each moment. Thus, this is the meditative practice: to attempt to notice continuously when we are thinking versus when we are completely present, immersed in the sensual experience of sight, sound, and smell in each moment, without any sense of subject or object.

It is preferable to do this walking practice outside, in nature, where there are many stimuli, but you can walk inside as well.

1. At first, notice your body movement, just as instructed in the previous walking meditation. Walk at a modest pace, or a fairly slow stroll.

2. Now, close your eyes for intervals of 15 seconds as you walk, glancing periodically so that you do not stumble. When the eyes are closed, notice as much sound as you can, listening to the farthest distance you can manage. When noticing sound, try not to identify it; just appreciate its basic elements: pitch, rhythm, volume, melody. Or simply notice it as a vibration. Sometimes it helps to stop walking occasionally when noticing sound, and then to slowly continue the pace.

3. Each time you open your eyes, try to notice as much as you can in the first visual impression, as if you were snapping a photograph. Again, try not to think about this experience, but rather work with your mental wide-angle lens, noticing the enormous variety in your visual field.

4. Occasionally when the eyes are closed, take a deep breath and notice if you are able to distinguish any special scents or odors. Soon you may discover a considerable variety, especially if you are in nature.

5. Follow steps 2–4 for the first half of your stroll. For the second half, please explore the following:

6. Keeping your eyes open from now on, allow your gaze to soften, sweeping from side to side. You will find that you tend to focus on things that catch your attention. Each time this happens, attempt to soften the focus and continue to sweep across the visual field. This experience of soft focus keeps us more in the present.

7. Using the same method, try to keep your hearing open at all times, allowing the sounds to flow in without focusing on any particular one. Sound is usually present as a constant stream. We tend to isolate particular sounds that attract us, but we also have the ability to be with the experience as if we were seated by a moving river, hearing its continuous rush.

8. Notice as well, without identifying it, anything that stimulates the olfactory sense. This is usually quite subtle, but much more apparent than most people realize.

9. Allow the total sensory experience—sight, sound, smell, touch, and taste—to enrich each moment. Notice how full, yet free, life feels when we are immersed in our senses. Notice, too, that this experience gives us a feeling of integration rather than the isolated feeling that often occurs when we are lost in thought.

This practice can be used and developed at all times, whether we are on our way to work, taking a lunch break, or simply moving from one place to another. It can be experienced moving or sitting, at home or on the road, with people or alone. The idea is simply to be aware of the sensory input, taking in as much as possible while allowing the thought process to rest as we concentrate solely on being organisms of pure receptivity.

This is a foundation practice for achieving devekut, becoming one with the Source of Life, in which we are able to let go of our self-consciousness and become vehicles of the divine will. We will see a number of devekut practices later in this book.

REFLECTIONS ON THE PSALMS (30–60 minutes)

> The rabbis taught: "Those who are humiliated by others, but who do not humiliate others, who listen to criticism without responding, do things out of love and have joy despite their sufferings, about them it is said: 'Those who love the Divine are like the sun in its full strength.'"
>
> Babylonian Talmud: *Shabbat* 88b

One of the most effective forms of meditation is the process of repetition and memorization. Repetition is used in many traditions in the form of mantras (Hindu and Buddhist), *wazifas* (Sufi), litanies (Christian), and prayer. Memorization is included to strengthen our concentration as well as to help free the mind from extraneous thoughts. It is a basic practice in many traditions, and has been a fundamental technique used in Judaism for thousands of years.

Memorization was so much a part of Judaism that an entire body of oral tradition was passed down from teacher to student for over a thousand years before it was ultimately recorded in writing. The Mishna, upon which the Talmud is based, means literally "to repeat," which is the practice required to sustain an oral tradition. In the days of the Talmud, two thousand years ago, individuals had prodigious memories and could quote entire volumes word for word.

Memory continues to be a major part of traditional Jewish education. Young students memorize dozens of pages of oral tradition and vast amounts of Torah and Talmud. This practice turns out to be a useful contemplative technique. It is especially helpful for people who are plagued by a busy, unruly monkey mind that constantly swings from one thought to another.

Many options are available to us for memory work, but the most universal source is the Book of Psalms. In Psalms we find a wide range of emotional expression, marvelous poetry, and a language that is deeply devotional. Memorizing lines from the psalms is not only beneficial in our meditative practice, it also has the side benefit of elevating our potential for meaningful prayer. Something transformative occurs when we repeat these words over and over; they begin to resonate on their own, and this has a mysterious effect upon our souls.

Try it and see what happens:

1. Ask yourself a meaningful spiritual question. Then glance at verses from Psalms in your own text, or at the short phrases from Psalms in the appendix. Pick one verse that seems to call to you.

2. Write this verse on a card, first in English, and then—if you have elementary Hebrew skills—in Hebrew. English will work fine in terms of meaning and content, but the poetry lies in the Hebrew version.

3. Learn the verse by heart, repeating it over and over for about 10 minutes.

4. Find this verse in a Book of Psalms. Read over the entire psalm. (You will probably have a different English version than is recorded in the appendix, but it will be close. There are dozens of versions in English.)

5. Sit quietly, contemplating the meaning of the psalm and how it speaks to you. Now, without looking, see if you can remember the verse that you memorized a few minutes ago. If not, look at it, write it down again, and repeat it a number of times.

6. Repeat steps 1–5 with a new verse from Psalms. At various moments during the process, see if you can recall the original verse that you memorized. Do this over and over again with three different verses.

7. When your time is up, put everything away and go on with your day, but set an alarm to buzz 1 or 2 hours from

now. When the alarm goes off, see if you can remember the three verses. For any that you cannot remember, look once again at the card you have written and spend a minute memorizing it.

8. Memory depends on repetition and time. When learning entirely new things, we often forget at least half of what we learn within a few hours. This is why it is important to refresh the memory every couple of hours. After a while, the memorized material stays with us and then only needs to be refreshed every few days. In this way, quite a few verses can be memorized in a fairly short time.

For those who are ambitious in the memory technique, it is recommended that you learn as many psalms as you wish. If one is not enough, learn two or more. Some people memorize all one hundred and fifty psalms. This is an excellent project and pays rich rewards in many ways.

However, be careful not to allow your ambitions to cloud your basic meditative practice of equanimity. Do not have expectations for total recall to last forever. Treat memorization as an end in itself; the primary value comes from concentrating the mind. The amount of time you are able to remember something should not be judged. If you forget a line, simply return and memorize it over again, without self-criticism. This relaxed approach allows a sense of freedom in the entire process, and then it becomes a joy rather than a burden. Joy is one of the key foundation stones of Jewish meditative practice. Relax. Have fun with this practice.

PSYCHO-SPIRITUAL JOURNALING

(15–45 minutes)

A Mishna teaches: "These are the things of
which a person enjoys the interest of the reward
in this world, while the principal remains in the
world to come. They are: honoring one's mother
and father, practicing lovingkindness, receiving
guests, making peace between people, and
above all studying Torah."

Babylonian Talmud: *Kiddushin* 40a

Journaling has become a popular practice in recent
years. It usually consists of writing down one's
thoughts, dreams, aspirations, and experiences. Often it
helps us reveal an inner dimension that initially may have
been difficult to articulate. It is also an excellent tool with
which to probe our psychological makeup. When done
skillfully, journaling is a remarkable way to discover parts of
ourselves that we never knew existed. This process lends
itself to a specific kind of inquiry that is of interest to
spiritual explorers: I call it psycho-spiritual journaling.

Psycho-spiritual journaling allows us to dwell on soul
levels, inquire into mystical realms, and profoundly
experience other dimensions of reality. The primary
difference between this form and the typical journaling
experience is in the subject matter. In psycho-spiritual
journaling, one is always directed to the kabbalistic level of
atzilut—the spiritual domain.

For journaling we need paper, preferably a bound book
of blank pages, and a writing instrument that is comfortable,
smooth, and fluid. A pen or a mechanical pencil is best,
because normal pencils wear down too quickly. The main
thrust in this kind of writing is to develop a rhythm in
which the words flow out unconstrained by the editorial
part of the mind. When Jewish mystics did this technique in
the past, it was called "automatic writing."

Some of the best advice for journaling has been written by Natalie Goldberg, a leader in the field. In her book *Wild Mind*, she lists four "rules" for good journaling:

1. Keep your hand moving.
2. Lose control.
3. Be specific.
4. Don't think.

The main idea in journaling is to let go of the logical mind so that no limits are placed on what flows from the pen. There are no concerns regarding grammar and punctuation—nobody is going to grade your effort; indeed, nobody else is likely to see it. Therefore, you are completely free.

Now, please find a comfortable position for writing, pick one of the following subjects, and let yourself go, continuing for as long as you wish, up to 45 minutes. If you finish before that time, you may choose another subject from the list or you may elect to sit quietly for the remainder of the time.

Subjects for psycho-spiritual journaling:

1. Imagine that you have a soul that existed before you were born. Imagine that this soul was able to communicate with other souls. Imagine discussing with these other souls what you intend to do, or what you need to do when you take on a living body. Let them tell you what their intentions are as well. Begin.

2. Imagine that you are able to visit with angels. Describe the setting; describe what the angels look like to you. Pick out one angel and have a conversation with it. Ask it anything you wish and discover what it has to say. Begin.

3. Imagine that you are in a garden and that other creatures are living in this garden. Normally they are invisible, but today you can see them. Describe what they look like. Introduce yourself to different creatures and have a conversation with each. Begin.

4. Imagine that you are standing at the gates of heaven, observing what happens as souls pass in either direction. Describe the scene and how you feel about it. Stop some of the souls and engage them in conversation, asking them whatever you wish. Begin.

5. Imagine that you can communicate directly with the Source of Life. Ask it about yourself—where you come from, why you are here. Ask it to tell you about the secret of life. Ask it any other questions you wish. Begin.

6. Imagine that you have become completely enlightened. What does it feel like? How do you relate to others? What is the world like at this time? What can you do as an enlightened being that you could not do before? Imagine doing these things and describe the experience. Begin.

7. Think of a difficult life experience you have had. Consider all the variables that allowed this experience to occur, including the backgrounds of all the people involved. Imagine how the experience affected your soul and the souls of the others. Assume you are able to understand the cosmic design around this event. Describe all these possibilities. Begin.

8. Imagine that you can be in direct contact with someone who has died. Describe what the person looks like to you at this time. Ask him to describe his present situation. What it is like where she is? Ask the person to tell you about the journey of death. Write down this conversation. Begin.

9. Imagine that you can speak with the Source of Love. Describe the presence of divine love. Ask it to tell you about the secrets of love, and how one goes about attaining the fullness of the loving experience. Begin.

10. Reflect on your life the last few weeks. What seems to be going well for you? What seems to be in need of adjustment? Imagine you have the power to change two or

three things in your life. Describe them in some detail. How would you go about changing them?

11. Describe to yourself the ideal life style you imagine for yourself with regard to work, relationships, personal time, spiritual exploration, creativity, productivity, wealth, and use of free time. Do this now. When finished, go to #12.

12. Seeing yourself through the eyes of God, so to speak, understanding your potential and purpose from the perspective of divine awareness, describe the perfect life for yourself. Notice the difference between the view of the perfect life from the perspective of God and the ideal life you perceived for yourself in #11.

Please do as many journaling entries as you can before working with the kabbalistic meditations at the end of this book. Many of the suggestions above provide seed material for the visualizations introduced later. Once you have experienced these journaling experiences on your own, the guided meditations you will encounter later will be significantly enhanced. Thus, it is highly recommended to come back to this exercise frequently to develop the skills you will use later in the kabbalistic visualizations.

KAVANNAH AND CONTINUITY PRACTICE
(30–45 minutes)

> The secret of the Torah is not the Kabbalah, for that is already written in texts and anyone can learn it by studying with a partner; so it can hardly be called secret. The real meaning of secret regarding the Torah refers to what is revealed to individuals according to their level.
>
> The Piasetsner: Rabbi Kalonymos Kalmish Shapira

One of the goals of spiritual practice is to integrate the inner with the outer. At first we may need to withdraw from our busy lives in order to nourish the soul, but the aim of almost all inner work is to find a way to maintain our spiritual balance in every situation we encounter. Thus, one of the most useful techniques is called "continuity" practice, which means attempting to stay in meditative consciousness throughout the day. In Judaism this is known as *kavannah*, being aware of the underlying intention of all our actions.

The secret of continuity practice—being present in the moment—is to pay great attention to the fine detail in whatever we are doing. We draw upon all our senses in this experience.

1. Whatever you are doing, become visually aware. See the variety of color, shape, light, shadow, texture, contrast, and background. Look at what you are doing and everything around you through the eyes of an artist about to paint the scene.

2. Become aurally aware. Hear the sounds of your movement, of everything in your vicinity. Listen for the subtlest sound you can distinguish nearby or in the distance. Notice the quality of the sound, its rhythm, pitch, loudness, how it blends with other sounds. There is an enormous

variety of sound almost all the time. Most of it we miss. Pay close attention.

3. Notice odors, scents, the smell of materials, packaging, bodies, plants, earth, food. Many subtleties of our olfactory sense are subliminal. Try to bring this awareness into consciousness.

4. Experience the tactile sensations. Feel the elemental quality of each touch, the degree to which it is soft, hard, sharp, blunt, round, rough, warm, or cool. Notice the experience of your own body, how it moves, its posture, how the muscles stretch and contract; notice the feel of clothes against the skin and the weight of the body on the chair or the floor.

5. Notice how you are feeling as you engage in various activities. Are you tense, relaxed, rushed, sad, anxious, alert, tired, frustrated, angry, happy? Notice that your mood often changes when tasks change.

6. Most important, try to be aware of your thoughts. Are you daydreaming most of the time, thinking about being somewhere else, planning for the future, reviewing a recent event, trying to relive events repeatedly by continually substituting new scenarios, remembering old experiences, conjuring up fantasies? Notice that when you are thinking, it is almost impossible to experience any of the sensations described above.

Using this guidance for kavannah, we can attempt to be aware of each moment in its totality. We soon discover that when we are caught in our thoughts, we are not present; when we are fully present, our minds are clear and receptive.

One can do continuity practice in any situation, whether at home, doing housework, shopping, driving to work, walking in a crowd, lying on the beach, or sitting quietly in nature. Wherever we are, we can bring added awareness to each moment.

Starting right now, without waiting, try to heighten your awareness of the senses and your mind state. Do this for the entire 30–45 minutes with as much concentration as you are able to bring to each moment. Although this is a set period of practice, ideally we attempt to practice continuity—to sharpen the kavannah—continuously, and indeed we try to take as much of this ongoing practice as possible into everyday experience.

This is one of the most important meditative practices in one's repertoire. It is easy to describe and relatively easy to experience, but extraordinarily difficult to maintain, for the mind is constantly sweeping us into a state of forgetfulness. Do your best to stay aware. Gently keep reminding yourself to be present. This ultimately will become a lifelong practice, and the rewards are well worth the effort.

CHESED: THE LOVINGKINDNESS
MEDITATION (30–45 minutes)

> The Lord passed in front of [Moses] and
> proclaimed: The Lord God is merciful and
> gracious, long suffering, abundant in goodness
> and truth, and sustains mercy for the multitudes,
> constantly forgiving iniquity and
> transgressions...
>
> Exodus 34:7

Forgiveness—asking for it and giving it—is a basic Jewish practice. On the High Holy Days, Jews perform rituals and prayers that beg God for forgiveness for acts between themselves and others as well as between themselves and the Source of Life. This act of contrition has a deep healing effect and is used in many traditions.

The following meditation has extraordinary power to heal psychic wounds, release negative energies, and bring a new sense of inner peace. In Buddhist tradition, this is called a *metta* (friendship) meditation. In Judaism, it could be called the *chesed* (lovingkindness)meditation.

This is an excellent meditation to use late at night, just before going to sleep. It is one of the few meditations that is actually recommended for doing in bed, as it is a wonderful way to fall asleep. Read over the following guidelines a few times so that you understand the sequence of the meditation and have it roughly memorized. (Obviously, if doing this in bed, you will want to follow the meditation on your own without referring to the book.)

1. Assume a comfortable, relaxed position. If lying down, do not assume your normal sleeping pose. If you usually sleep on your side or stomach, then do this meditation on your back, or vice versa.

2. Notice the movement of your chest as it rises and falls with your breath. Allow yourself to reflect on the events of the previous week.

3. If an event arises in which you realize you have acted unskillfully, or in which someone else may have hurt your feelings, allow that to be a focus of your meditation. If nothing specific arises, then this meditation will be more general.

4. Think to yourself: *If I have harmed anyone or anything, directly or indirectly, intentionally or unconsciously, I ask for your forgiveness.* Allow images to arise of the previous week, or of any time in your life, and visualize asking for forgiveness.

5. Now think to yourself: *If anyone has harmed me, directly or indirectly, intentionally or unconsciously, I offer you my forgiveness.* Once again, allow images to arise for the previous week or any time in your life, and visualize offering forgiveness to the best of your ability.

6. Think to yourself: *May I be happy.* [Imagine special, happy moments in your life.] *May I be peaceful.* [Imagine peaceful moments in your life.] *May I be free.* [Imagine moments of freedom in your life.] (Happiness, peacefulness, and freedom are used for this exercise; however, you may select any three attributes with which you wish to resonate, for example, lovingkindness, serenity, grace, wisdom, gentleness.)

7. Think of someone you dearly love and visualize this person as clearly as you can. Think to yourself: *Just as I wish to be happy, may you be happy. Just as I wish to be peaceful, may you be peaceful. Just as I wish to be free, may you be free.* Each time you mention a quality, remember your own life experiences with that quality. It is very important not simply to say the words, but actually to visualize and feel the experience.

8. Think of someone about whom you do not have strong feelings and repeat the phrase for step 7 *(Just as I wish to be happy...).*

9. Visualize someone about whom you have negative feelings and once again repeat step 7. You can repeat this over and over with different individuals for as long as you wish.

10. Visualize people in your local community and repeat step 7 for each individual you can bring into your awareness.

11. Visualize a broad segment of people as a group, any category you wish, such as all of a selected minority, all who suffer from cancer, all who are hungry, all who are in pain, and send a general prayer to all of them: *May you be happy, may you be peaceful, may you be free.*

12. Let your prayers extend out to the farthest reaches of the universe, to the limits of your imagination: *May all beings be happy, may all beings be peaceful, may all beings be free.*

If lying in bed, at some point in the meditation you will know that it is time to assume your normal sleeping pose. You will find that this process done regularly will have highly positive effects on your sleep and on your general sense of well-being. This meditation has no limits on the amount of time you can use it, or where, or when. It is always beneficial.

For anyone taking a one-day retreat, this is a marvelous way to complete the day, to nourish your soul with light and love, and to experience the healing that comes through sending your love and goodwill throughout the universe.

MEDITATIVE PRAYER (30–60 minutes)

> The service of the heart is prayer, that is, to nullify one's self-identity and to merge with the Infinite Nothingness.
>
> Rabbi Nachman of Breslov, *Likutey Moharan* 22:9

Prayer is often a difficult practice for modern people. The main obstacle for most of us is the question that immediately comes to mind: To what or to whom am I praying?

Interestingly, whenever we are under extreme stress and feeling helpless, when a family member is suffering a life-threatening illness or injury, we often discover that prayer comes fairly easily. Sometimes this prayer is prefaced with, "I don't know what power exists that can save my loved one's life, but whatever it is, please help us, please don't let him/her die, please..."

Most of us experience this kind of supplication at one time or another in our lives. When we have no place to turn, our natural inclination is to call out to the unknown. It happens spontaneously and with great force.

One of the reasons many of us have problems with the practice of prayer is that prayers have been systematically compiled for us so that a community wishing to pray together can be organized for ritual gatherings. Reading prayers out of a book may capture our thoughts, but the emotional and spiritual potential of these prayers often evaporates in the aridity of the intellectual experience. Today, many people confuse reading liturgical prayers with prayer itself. This is a sad mistake, because the primordial source of prayer rests deep within us. Moreover, each truly heartfelt prayer is uniquely one's own.

Genuine prayer transcends the rational mind; it dwells in unknown and mystical realms. On that level, one never asks who or what is at the center of the universe. In the depths of authentic prayer, intellectual and philosophical concerns are put aside. Prayer is an emotive experience to which one's total being must be committed.

As a meditative and contemplative practice, prayer is enormously powerful. Recently, people involved in medicine have been exploring the efficacy of prayer. In his book *Healing Words*, Dr. Larry Dossey presents a number of scientific studies that show evidence of the healing potency of prayer.

Nobody knows how prayer works, but most cultures share a belief that when our essential nature is fervently expressed through the medium of prayer, something happens—something reverberates throughout the universe.

There are three basic types of prayer: invocation/praise, supplication/request, and thanksgiving.

The following exercises are designed to break through negative experiences you may have had with prayer and to open new pathways of communing with the unknown. You will need paper and something to write with. Please write by hand, as this exercise will not work as well if you use a typewriter or computer. Part of the experience is to physically feel the texture of the writing, the movement of the hands and arms, and the connection of the pencil or pen as it flows over the paper. Please do no more than two or three exercises during any single meditation period. Now, get your writing materials, and let us begin.

1. Write a letter to God (10–30 minutes).

   a. Describe the image you have of God.
   b. Describe how you feel about God.
   c. Describe your feelings about the world.
   d. Describe your concerns about the world.
   e. Describe what you need for yourself.

2. Be God and write a letter to yourself from God's perspective (10–30 minutes).

   a. Describe your good points.
   b. Describe your weak points.
   c. Describe what God expects of you.

3. Write a letter to God with three major requests and explain why you feel that you should have them (10–30 minutes).

   a. How would receiving them benefit you?
   b. How would they benefit the world?
   c. What price would you pay for each?

4. Write a letter from God to you regarding the requests in number 3, responding to each of your points (10–30 minutes).

5. Imagine that you are three years old, cradled in the arms of your mother. Using your nondominant hand (if you are right-handed, write this letter with your left hand), write a letter to your mother describing your needs in great detail. Write another letter to your father. Notice any similarities and any differences that you discover between the two letters (10–30 minutes for each letter).

6. Imagine the presence of someone who is deceased— someone you knew. Write a letter to yourself from the perspective of this deceased family member or friend covering the following points (30–60 minutes):

   a. What is it like where he or she is?
   b. What advice would that person give you?
   c. What can she or he teach you about:

   - relationship?
   - love?
   - the meaning of life?
   - your specific purpose in life?

7. Imagine that you have died and are viewing a videotape of major events in your life. Write about these events one at a time, and comment on them from the perspective of afterlife (30–60 minutes).

8. Imagine that you have just come from a doctor's office with the diagnosis of a terminal illness that gives you only one year to live. Write about how you would live the last year of your life, assuming that you will not suffer any pain and that when death arrives, it will come swiftly and silently (30–60 minutes).

Each of these practices opens inner gates. After doing one or more of the above practices, open a prayer book to any page and read a few lines. Sometimes the words will be directly to the point of your practice; at other times they will seem wholly irrelevant. When written prayers connect with your inner space, you can touch new depths. If this happens, read and repeat the important line over and over again in your mind and your heart. This is what praying is really about.

On the other hand, if nothing connects, then continue with your exercises aside from the prayer book. These exercises warm the heart; they speak a language of the soul, and just doing them elicits a prayerful state of being.

Prayer cannot be accomplished in a rote fashion, nor can we count on being raised to the heights each time we pray. But we can learn to gain new accessibility to the soul by performing exercises such as these until we have found our inner voice that prays in its own language. It is then that we truly experience the power of prayer and, through it, connect with a new reality.

CONTEMPLATIVE STUDY (30–60 minutes)

> A holy word of Torah or prayer cleaves its way
> through the heavens until it reaches a special
> place, where it awaits nightfall. When the soul
> ascends [in the night], it seizes those holy words
> and presents them to God.
>
> *Zohar* 121b

One of the most often used meditative practices in Judaism is to contemplate inspirational ideas and wisdom teachings, especially those that have withstood the test of time. Reading contemplatively is not the same as reading for entertainment. In contemplative reading, we tend to dwell for a long time on a few words; usually there is no plot, and the thoughts that are provoked are often wide-ranging. At times, we enter realms that seem completely unrelated to the subject of the material that was read. Many inspirational books are never read to completion. They are opened to any page and frequently the reader does not go beyond the selected page for that day.

Many inspirational books are available. Some people have their own favorite poetry or spiritual teachers. In Judaism, there is a wide variety of classical texts as well as scriptural writings that draw us deeply into a contemplative mode. Some of those works are listed at the back of this book.

The key is to read slowly, chew over the words, dwell in the imagination. Treat this kind of writing as if it were a way for souls to communicate—that is, the soul of the writer, that of the source of inspiration, the many souls that have contemplated this idea, and your soul. From this perspective, our entire life can turn on a phrase, our view of reality may hinge on a thought.

Contemplative reading is not only inspirational during the day, it is also an excellent way to prepare for sleep. You will soon notice a remarkable difference between going to bed after watching television and the sleep that comes after meditation or a contemplative, inspirational experience. Thus, each evening, when you have grown tired and are preparing for sleep, spend a short time reflecting on an inspirational line or two. One of the best sources of inspiration is the *TANACH*, which includes: the Torah—the Five Books of Moses; the writings of the Prophets, which include Joshua, Judges, Samuel, Kings, Isaiah, Jeremiah, Ezekiel and the Twelve Prophets; and the Holy Writings ,which include Psalms, Proverbs, Job, the Song of Songs, Ruth, Lamentations, Ecclesiastes, Esther, Daniel, Ezra/Nehemiah, and Chronicles. All of these are contained in one large volume that can be kept handy.

Reading the *TANACH* is often a challenging task. Most people are inclined to read the literal meaning of the words. When this is done, the Torah often reads like a historical document that is archaic, primitive, and, in some instances, irrelevant. The classical approach to reading Torah, however, suggests that there are four primary ways to understand these writings. These four ways form an acronym called *PaRDeS*. The word *pardes* means "orchard," and is sometimes translated as "garden." It is made up of the Hebrew letters *peh, resh, dalet,* and *samech.*

The letter peh stands for *peshat,* which means "the literal interpretation." Although this is the simplest and most natural way to read anything, it is also one of the most demanding. From this perspective, the words are describing what actually happened; the words mean exactly what they say. When the words describe something that coincides with our normal experience, we project our perception into the reading and assume we understand what it is saying. In fact, the material we are reading may be referring to an entirely different experience. On the other hand, when we read something that is beyond our experience, we tend to be wary, disbelieving it or rejecting it outright, whereas it might be teaching us a new way to perceive reality. In either instance, the peshat, or literal meaning, may bring to us new knowledge that heretofore was inaccessible.

The letter resh stands for the word *remez,* meaning a "hint." The remez approach suggests that we can read everything as an allusion to some deeper meaning. Just as we read an allegory or parable not for itself but for the message it contains, so, too, we are able to read every inspirational work as if it were teaching us something well beyond our normal perspective of the world. In other words, this is the idea that everything we see and everything that happens is a metaphor of universal principles.

The letter dalet stands for *drosh,* which is a way of comparing one teaching with another to discover important messages. It is as if some wisdom teachings were encoded in a way that makes them unattainable unless we are able to connect them with other, completely different wisdom teachings. The drosh approach utilizes a wide range of oral tradition to introduce perspectives and techniques of interpretation that add a multitude of lenses through which any teaching acquires an entirely new hue.

Finally, the letter samech stands for *sod,* which means "secret." This is the unrevealed and mysterious level, the level of the Kabbalah. The sod assumption is that every wisdom teaching is actually a veil that contains within it the secrets of the universe. Although the teaching itself may embrace enormous wisdom on a peshat, remez, or drosh level, the sod perspective is that hidden deep within is a kernel of truth upon which the entire universe revolves.

There are two ways to approach the sod level: (1) to be acquainted with the language of the Kabbalah so as to understand conceptual categories into which various teachings fit; and (2) to be attuned to one's inner guide, which is the gateway to intuitive understanding. Even though many people are unfamiliar with the language of the Kabbalah, they can still appreciate kabbalistic insight by accessing the core of their own central awareness.

The practice of contemplative study works with a few sentences at a time:

1. Read the literal meaning. Try to imagine that you are a participant at the event about which you are reading; experience what it feels like to be present at this event. What does this new perspective mean to you once you have set aside your modern critical and judgmental mind? Pretend to yourself that this was a meaningful and moving event that you personally experienced. Relive it over and over in your imagination.

2. Now, consider that this message actually represents something else; it is a teaching about one of life's truths. Imagine that a teacher whom you deeply respect has said these words to you and you must discover a profound message within. Look for the hidden message.

3. Imagine that you can take the words apart, introducing new ideas by manipulating the letters of the words or by reversing the apparent meaning through word substitution. Change the scene entirely in any way you wish. Keep bringing in new possibilities that may even develop a thought that directly opposes the literal meaning. Let your imagination have free rein and see what happens.

4. Assume that a universal truth applies to every aspect of creation, that every molecule has a spark of holiness, and that wherever we look we can find a reflection of the Divine. Sometimes it is hidden in the most obscure places; sometimes we can experience its presence without understanding how it has manifested in this way, but we know for certain that it is here. Approach your reading from this perspective, knowing that the divine spark is present in everything, and experience how this viewpoint opens new insights.

5. Repeat steps 1–4 each time you come to a new thought or idea in your reading.

6. When you are about ready to quit, please do one more thing. Stop your reading, close the book, and sit quietly, eyes closed for a few minutes. Allow a question to

arise, something that is bothering you at this time. Let the question form as if you were able to ask the wisest person you know. Once the question is clear, open the book at random, let your finger fall on a paragraph, and read it carefully, following steps 1–4, specifically receptive to the possibility of some kind of answer to your question. See what happens.

Contemplative study is an extraordinarily rich practice. The most difficult passages are often the most rewarding when we become absorbed in them. This is an excellent and often inspirational method of attuning to other realms of reality; it usually touches the soul on a very deep level.

HITBODEDUT: ALONE WITH GOD
(30–60 minutes)

> The Rabbis taught: "A person should always consider that one's rewardable acts and one's punishable acts are equally balanced, so that any single rewardable act will tip the scales to one's favor, while any punishable act will tip the scales the other way, [thus making every single act crucial.]"
>
> Babylonian Talmud: *Kiddushin* 40b

One of the best-known forms of Jewish meditative prayer is called *hitbodedut*. It comes from the Hebrew root *bodad* (to be isolated), and it means to seclude oneself—in essence, to be alone with God. It is a very simple technique that is also quite effective. One merely speaks out whatever happens to be on one's mind to the Creator of the universe.

It is important to be alone so that you can use your voice without worrying about others listening in. You can do the meditation at home if you feel comfortable there, but it is often recommended that one be in nature when doing hitbodedut. The most famous Hasidic leader who used and taught this method—Rabbi Nachman of Breslov—suggested that people should go into the woods, especially at night, to do this practice.

Many people shy away from speaking directly to God; they often feel embarrassed, unworthy, or unbelieving. The important aspect of this method is that anything becomes grist for the mill. An integral part of the hitbodedut practice is to speak out loud—do not merely think the thought. In kabbalistic terms, actually speaking the words carries much more emotional content than thinking the words. In Jewish mysticism, prayer needs to be articulated; the combination of sounds will reverberate throughout the universe and have more impact than thought waves.

When you feel like communing directly with the Divine, hitbodedut is an excellent method. Although it is often done standing or walking, you can also sit quietly to enhance the inner power of the meditation. If you are at home, please try to find a place where you will not be interrupted and where others in the house cannot hear you.

1. Begin with the basic sitting technique: relaxed, eyes closed. Try to sit fairly straight without effort. Breathe normally. Notice the rising and falling of the chest with the breath.

2. Now, find your own words to express one of the following ideas:

> Whatever is at the center of creation, whatever you call yourself, if there is any way that you can do this, please help me believe that I can really communicate with you.

> God, I am not really sure who or what you are; please help me feel your presence.

3. If you are unable to experience anything at all, you can either continue asking for help, or you can literally pretend; use your imagination, and imagine being cradled or hugged by a warm, loving entity of some type. Imagine that you are in the arms of pure love. In essence, pretend that you are talking to a loving source, speaking your heart's deepest secrets, asking for whatever you need to get an inner healing. Being held like this, close, secure, loved, let yourself speak out in your own words; let your heart flow with whatever is in it. You will discover along the way that although this process may begin as an exercise in pretending, it will ultimately become an experience of great healing—it really works! Try it.

4. When you are ready, please finish a request with something like the following:

a. Oh, I want to be free—please help me be free.
b. I need to feel better—please help me feel better.
c. If only I could have peace—please help me find peace.

Once you have completed this exercise, even though it may feel strange at first, simply notice brief memories of the experience that may arise over the next few days. Try to do this hitbodedut meditation at least once a week for a few months, and in between the practice sessions; keep noticing how the mind occasionally turns to the memories. Eventually, barriers will begin to fall and you will most likely find greater comfort in the practice. Slowly it will bring you closer to connecting with something mysterious, which will lead to a letting go of some boundaries so that you will be able to have a sense of greater peace. This is a major practice for ultimately attaining devekut, merging with the Divine, and is highly recommended.

Jewish Retreats

Rabbi Huna said: "If a person is in the desert and does not know which day is Shabbat, he counts six days and observes the seventh." Chayah bar Rav says: "The person should observe the first day as Shabbat, and then count six days." In what are they disagreeing? Rabbi Huna believes that it should be similar to the creation of the world [in which there were six days and the seventh was Shabbat], while Chayah bar Rav believes that it should be similar to the creation of Adam (who was created in the hours just before Shabbat, and thus celebrated his first day of existence as Shabbat].

Babylonian Talmud: *Shabbat* 69b

Judaism is built upon two fundamental wisdom teachings: (1) There is no separation between Creator and Creation, and (2) we need to "rest" from our normal, worldly activity if we wish to appreciate the truth of existence. Each of these teachings is in symbiotic relationship with the other. We learn the profound truth of the non-duality of creation when we are able to temporarily withdraw from our mundane lives. When we experience the true meaning of ultimate oneness, our everyday lives take on an entirely new meaning.

The Experience of Oneness

The first teaching, that of non-separation, is expressed in the quintessential Jewish prayer, the *Shema*, which interpreted mystically says, "Listen carefully at the core of your being, the part of you that yearns to go straight to the Source of Life, the transcendent unknowable God and all that we see in the material world surrounding us are, in fact, one and the same." It is all one. This truth is so important, according to Jewish law, that we are required to repeat it to ourselves at least twice a day so that we remember it. This means, in literal terms, to actually say the words *Shema Yisrael, Adonoy Elohaynu, Adonoy Ehad*, every morning and every evening.

In esoteric terms, the admonishment to repeat the Shema implores us to sink into the realization of the truth of non-duality, to keep these things "in your heart…when sitting in your home, walking on the way, lying down, or standing up…" In other words, we must rest in the understanding of oneness not just twice a day, but all of our waking hours as we engage in every activity of life.

Clearly this is not easy to do. Mundane life rapidly overwhelms us. Our minds are so complex and work so fast, we quickly succumb into believing that reality is what we "think" it is—disparate, material, and solid. Despite the fact that our own thoughts continue to swiftly evaporate, proving that they were never "real" or concrete in the first place, we persist in believing whatever is happening in our minds at any particular moment.

Attempts to answer the essential inquiries of existence are the driving force of knowledge and understanding. The early philosophers sought common denominators, basic elements out of which all things arise, such as earth, air, fire, and water. After thousands of years we continue to seek the fundamental building blocks, now conceptualizing them as mysterious subatomic energy bundles called quarks. Nobody has ever seen a quark, but mathematical systems are built on such ideas.

Other ideas have metamorphosed over the years. Past beliefs in the nature of space and the continuous steady flow of time have transformed into current beliefs of relativity, a kind of flexibility of time and space, that is almost impossible for most of us to picture in our minds. Relativity is an idea that challenges us on the deepest levels, for it affects our bedrock of belief that reality is something that can be seen, touched, measured, and eventually known with the proper tools. We are now taught that things work very differently than we can even imagine, and reality has multiple levels that rapidly transcend the grasp of human consciousness.

For example, we are no longer certain that there are solid building blocks upon which reality is constructed. At times, subatomic energy has the properties of little particles; at other times it seems to have properties of waves constantly in motion. More mysterious, when we set up experiments to look for particles, we find them; yet, using the same experimental method, if we are looking for waves instead, that's what we find. It is as if the observer influences the energy to behave in different ways. This has led modern science to conclude that we cannot separate a subject from an object, for the very act of observation affects that which is being observed.

This idea of inseparability casts an entirely new light on how we work with the primordial questions of what, how, where, when, and why as applied to the meaning of life, for we are compelled to reflect upon the source and nature of the question itself. Who, indeed, is asking the question? If there is no ultimate separation between subject and object, then we have a loop in which the answer and the question are intrinsically interconnected. Thus, rather than looking outward, as if the solutions to life's mysteries are somewhere to be found out there, we are being invited to look inward, to explore the unique energy of the creative urge that arises within each of us every moment of our lives.

There is yet another change arising in the way we look at things these days, far subtler than ramifications of the notion of inseparability. This change arises from the revelation that we can no longer precisely measure anything. The tools of measurement have their own limitations and those who are measuring, of course, have theirs as well. When the measuring stick is composed of the same elements as what it is used to measure, clear limitations arise. A measuring stick cannot measure itself! Moreover, the thickness of an electron is too great to measure another electron. Even worse, everything in the universe is constantly in motion, so there is never a static motion to measure it. Add to this yet another difficulty: That which is being measured reacts differently than when it is not being measured! Given all this (and there is more), we end up with never being able to measure anything exactly, and we can only come up with mere approximations.

As all measurement is approximate to some degree, then so-called ultimate truth is always unknown. That is to say, knowledge has limits. Not only are there things that we do not know, far more disturbing is the fact that *there are some things that will never be known.* This is not something easy to swallow. Humans are intrinsically optimistic when it comes to knowledge. We believe that with enough effort and the right tools we will ultimately know everything that can be known. The closer we look into this area—what can be known—the more we discover how little there is that is knowable. Moreover, knowing splits into that which is intellectually understood and can be communicated, and the much larger arena of transcendental knowing that extends beyond reason and expression. Wisdom is not something that fits easily into books, but is rather built upon foundations of direct experience.

Both science and philosophy in many ways have circled back to elementary teachings given by mystics in many traditions. They teach that we can discover basic truths by simply resting in quiet reflection in a way that will lead us to a direct experience of our innate nature. This experience is one of inclusivity, wholeness, and oneness, an inner-connectedness of all things. When resting in this realization, we come to the essential Jewish wisdom teaching of *ehad,* oneness, the non-separation between Creator and Creation.

This idea of resting quietly in the moment to more fully appreciate the oneness of creation brings us to the second fundamental Jewish wisdom teaching: to take contemplative time each week specifically to explore the meaning of life. Indeed, this is such an important tenet of the tradition that it is one of the Ten Commandments: Remember and observe the Sabbath day.

The Sabbath and Holy Days

The admonition to remember and observe the Sabbath day is initially directed to the weekly Sabbath that in Judaism begins at sundown Friday night and ends at sundown Saturday night. But the idea of Sabbath also loosely refers to days that are referred to as *yomim tovim* (good days, or holy days), because the Jewish law applying to each of these days approximates, for the most part, similar restrictions as the Sabbath day itself. Thus, all holy days have the feel of a Sabbath, with only minor differences. This means that in addition to the fifty-two official Sabbath days every year, there are quite a few other times that require special attention. In addition to these are many minor holidays that have fewer restrictions, but still are treated with special awareness. Here are the best known of the major and minor holy days in the calendar, with brief descriptions of the special energy that can be the contemplative focus of each respective day.

ROSH HASHANA

Rosh Hashana is the Jewish New Year. It falls in September or early October. Its main theme is "remembrance" and "return" to the Source of Creation. This is the time of the blowing of the shofar, calling to God, and it is required for all Jews to hear a shofar on this day. The esoteric teaching is that the shofar confuses the "accuser," the negative energy left behind by our unskillful behavior. So this is a time of reprieve, when we may be able to modify in some way the consequences of our actions. This is a marvelous idea and has deep connotations. In a retreat, on this day, we would want to spend time reflecting on the past, noticing any actions, words, or thoughts that were regrettable, and committing ourselves to more skillful behavior in the future.

YOM KIPPUR

Yom Kippur comes on the tenth day after Rosh Hashana. The intervening days are called the Days of Awe, a time of deep introspection. Yom Kippur is known as the Sabbath of Sabbaths, recognized as the most awesome day of the year. On this day we observe a complete fast, including drinking water, from sundown to sundown. It is a perfect time for retreat. The Kabbalah describes this day as a time when we have God's ear, so to speak, and can change our destiny. It is the most awe-filled day of the year. Out of time and space, one dwells completely in intimacy with the Divine. It is the day the High Priest within each of us enters the Holy of Holies, also within each of us, and speaks a special name of God only spoken on this particular day. If the mind goes astray in this moment, we die, metaphorically.

The practice throughout the day of Yom Kippur is to imagine that the heavenly court is in the process of determining what one's coming year has in store, based on previous actions, speech, and thoughts. This contemplation is the focus of many hours of reflection about oneself, one's family, associates, friends, and the world in general.

SUKKOT

Sukkot comes four days after Yom Kippur. It is a seven-day holiday; the first and seventh days are special. The main *mitzvah* (commandment) of this period is to eat and sleep in a *sukkah*, a temporary dwelling with nothing overhead but a canopy of vegetation through which we can see the sky. On the esoteric level, the covering of the sukkah is equated with the skin of the Leviathan, the mythical monstrous beast upon which the righteous will feed at the time of messianic consciousness. The exposed sukkah carries a luminous reflection of the *Ohr Ein Sof,* the infinite light of awareness, and it draws visitors from other realms, particularly the patriarchs and matriarchs: Abraham, Sarah, Isaac, Rebecca, Jacob, Leah, Rachel, Moses, Tzipporah, Aaron, Joseph, and David. Each day different guests are welcomed to the sukkah.

For traditional Jews, Sukkot is a time of raising up four plants—an unopened, young palm branch *(lulav),* a citron-like fruit *(etrog),* three myrtle branches *(hadasim),* and two willow branches *(aravot)*—all held together in a special way in the hands. Waving these in the six directions—east, south, north, west, up, and down—symbolically represents all of space. This is done while chanting praises and supplications. It is an elementary ritual of thanksgiving for the harvest and prayers for the rains and good fortune required for harvest to come the following year. This is an extremely rich and colorful ceremony that touches participants and viewers in deep primordial places.

On retreat we would try to spend most of the day outdoors, and even sleep out at night if feasible. Each day, we would not only commune with nature, but we would also esoterically connect with the archetypal energies of the biblical characters, each of whom represents an energy within us. This is a great opportunity to work on our personal character. Obviously, it is a wonderful experience to construct and live in one's own sukkah. Any Jewish bookstore can provide information for those who may be interested. This is a time of great joy and thanksgiving for the bounty of our sustenance and all the gifts of life.

SHEMINI ATZERET

The seven-day festival of Sukkot ends in a three-day series of special days: *Hoshana Rabba, Shemini Atzeret,* and *Simcha Torah.* Hoshana Rabba is celebrated the last day of Sukkot, when each member of the congregation circles around the Torah seven times and finally beats on the ground five willow branches that have been bound together. It symbolizes a final resolve to purify oneself in preparation for the year to come.

Simcha Torah is a joyous day when the Torah scrolls are carried through the streets accompanied by a singing and dancing congregation. It is a day of profound transition, when the last paragraphs of the Torah are read in public, followed by the reading of the opening sentences of Genesis, which signifies yet another cycle of completion and new beginnings.

Shemini Atzeret, the day that falls between Hoshana Rabba and Simcha Torah, is one of the most profound days in the calendar for Jewish mystics. It is a holy day, treated in the same way as a regular Shabbat, but it has a secret connotation for kabbalists: It is the culmination of all of the activities of Rosh Hashana, the Days of Awe, Yom Kippur, the preparation days for Sukkot, the week of Sukkot itself, and Hoshana Rabba, a rich and exhausting period of three weeks—the most intense twenty-one days of the calendar. It indicates that we are about to begin the new cycle of the Torah tomorrow. There is a great heavenly sigh when God says, "Wow! That was wonderful. But it has been so much, let's you and I spend some time together alone, just you and me."

Shemini Atzeret is viewed in this context as the day of greatest intimacy with the Divine, a day of resting in each other's arms, a time of enormous contentment that we have done everything possible to perfect our relationship and now we simply enjoy each other's presence without any particular expectations. On retreat, this is a time of essential communion, trust, and relaxation. In an esoteric sense, we are lovers with the Divine, caressing and being caressed in every move, sensually enjoying the unfolding of each moment. It is a wonderful time of quiet recognition and simple, uncomplicated delight.

CHANUKKAH

Chanukkah is a festival of light that comes in December. It is an eight-day holiday well known for its symbolic *menorah* and the daily lighting of candles. On the first day one candle is lighted, and a new candle is added each day until we light eight candles on the eighth day. From a mystical perspective, Chanukkah has kabbalistic significance in that it comes at the darkest time of the year (in the Northern Hemisphere), and our lighting of candles at this time has cosmic implications of creation and renewal. Thus, our contemplative practice would be focused on creativity and optimism, what it takes to bring the light of wisdom into the darkness of ignorance. Notice that only one candle will illuminate a completely dark room. This is the metaphor of Chanukkah, a light that continues to grow from day to day.

TU B'SHEVAT

Tu b'Shevat comes in January or February. It is best known as the festival of trees and is a time when people plant trees in Israel. Mystically, it is a time when the will to live first finds expression, when the sap that will produce blossoms in springtime begins to flow. On retreat we spend extra time becoming very quiet so that we can explore the subtle quickening of our vital life force. Kabbalists celebrate this day by partaking in a special seder that includes a wide variety of fruits. Each fruit is classified in one of three categories, representing three of the Four Worlds of Kabbalah.

The lowest world of *assiyah* is represented by fruit that is protected in hard, inedible shells, like nuts. The next world of *yetzira* is represented by fruits with hard, inedible inner pits, like peaches or plums. Next, the world of *beriah* is represented by fruit that can be eaten whole, like grapes. Finally, the highest world of *atzilut* is too high for regular fruits. I usually represent it with maple syrup, which is the sap that the day is all about.

This seder uses four cups of wine, just like the Passover seder. But the difference is that red and white wine are mixed to represent the Four Worlds: full-bodied red at the bottom level of assiyah, mostly red on the second level of yetzira, mostly white on the third level of beriah, and full-bodied white on the top level of atzilut. Thus the seder celebrates different levels of creation manifesting, and our focus during the day is on developing our creative energies of rebirthing ourselves. (For more details on the Four Worlds, see descriptions in the upcoming section called Yihudim Chanting Meditation.)

PURIM

Purim comes in February or March. Traditionally, it is treated somewhat like carnival: People dress in outlandish costumes and imbibe intoxicating drinks. The Book of Esther is read at this time, describing when the Jewish nation was miraculously saved from total destruction. It is often noted that the Book of Esther at no time mentions any name of God in it. Yet, it represents one of the great miracles of the Jewish people. Thus, the mystery of the hidden God is a primary theme working on this day.

We are often grasping for the unknown and unknowable. When our minds take over, we can easily fall into despair. The secret of Purim is to come to grips with the possibilities of this hidden aspect of the Divine, which often is represented as holy sparks within hardened shells of mundane existence. We meditate on how to liberate these sparks in what seems to be in the face of overwhelming odds.

Many people equate the archenemy Haman in the time of Esther with the modern archenemy Hitler. Retreatants at Purim usually focus on the paradox of life; they contemplate the presence of evil in the world and the miracle of divine grace.

PASSOVER

Passover comes one month after Purim, in March or April. It is a seven-day holiday best known for the seder, which takes place on the first night and, for many, on the second night as well. Observant Jews have uncompromising dietary restrictions during the entire seven days. Next to Shabbat, Passover has the most complex body of Jewish law associated with it. The objective is to cleanse our lives of all *hametz* (leavening), which mystically is associated with pride and ego.

The story of the Exodus is retold at Passover to remind us of the relationship between enslavement and freedom. On retreat, we concentrate on understanding the areas in which we are enslaved—what has captured our minds, our beliefs, our sense of self-worth, our values—and how we might be able to attain new freedom. This is a perfect time to take the week and really explore the theme of freedom.

Passover has a wide spectrum of themes for personal reflection. It is not only a one- or two-day experience, but it also includes the thirty days leading up to it, and the forty-nine days of the Counting of the Omer that follow the first night of seder. Passover is an entire week of reflection, marked by the matzah we eat for seven (or eight) days. On the final night of the week, the esoteric celebration is focused on the crossing of the Red Sea, which symbolizes faith. Passover is the story of an escape when not really merited, of getting out of an impossible situation without deserving it.

SHAVUOT

Shavuot comes forty-nine days after the Passover seder, usually in May. It celebrates the giving of the Torah on Mount Sinai. Traditionally people study and learn the entire night of Shavuot, which is an excellent form of retreat. The mystical preparation for Shavuot occurs during the seven weeks between it and Passover. This is called the Counting of the Omer, and each of the forty-nine days is publicly enumerated during the first prayer of every day for seven weeks. The kabbalists added the idea that each of the forty-nine days represents an aspect of our being, our personality, and our deepest essence that needs to be fixed and uplifted so that when we receive the teachings of the Torah, we will be as pure and open as possible. Thus, cleansing and purification are the retreat practices of Counting the Omer, while the possibility of new levels of awareness is the retreat experience of Shavuot.

TISHA B'AV

Tisha b'Av occurs in the heat of summer, in late July or August. This is a fast day almost as strict as Yom Kippur. It is a day of observance that traditionally marks the destruction of the two temples of ancient Judaism. The temples represent the vehicle through which we can communicate with God. Thus, Tisha b'Av is a day of mourning that this communication is now much more difficult—almost impossible. On retreat, this is a time to reflect on the gap between our spiritual essence and our mundane lives, with the hope that we can close this gap and attain an expanded level of consciousness, sometimes called messianic consciousness.

ROSH HODESH

Rosh Hodesh is the day each month of the new moon. It is treated as a special day by kabbalists, for the moon is viewed esoterically as the gathering place of souls. It is also the point when the quality of *gevurah*, constriction, gives way to *chesed*, expansion. The kabbalists look at midnight each day in the same way, as the end of the darkening process and the beginning of the enlightening cycle. Women also celebrate Rosh Hodesh in the context of moon cycles as a time of renewal and fertility, with great hope for possibilities unfolding anew.

Holy Days and the Contemplative Lifestyle

The meditative experiences of Sabbaths and holy days, the daily cycles of ordinary Jewish life, in quiet appreciation of the divine presence, in prayer, in study, in giving extraordinary care to and concern about mundane activities, in careful management of food, in acts of chesed (lovingkindness), in *tzeddakah* (right-minded charity), in expressions of gratitude, and in ongoing awareness of social consciousness, gives us an overview of the world of Judaism that reveals an extraordinarily rich selection of opportunities for expanding consciousness. When seen through meditative eyes, the possibilities are almost beyond comprehension, for all the major and most of the minor holidays in Judaism can be dramatically enhanced through meditation and silent retreats.

The power of the cycles of the Jewish calendar cannot be overemphasized. The constant reminder to look into life more deeply keeps one in a high state of alertness. There is a connection to the outside with the phase of the moon, the seasons, the times of sunrise and sunset, and the rains. On the inside, we are constantly asked to reflect on our motives, intentions, the nature of our actions, our communications, our relationships, our attention to detail, and our integrity. On the mystical plane, we are continuously being reminded of hidden meanings, the messages in events, the mysteries of unplanned contacts with individuals, the realization that there are no accidents, the amazing little miracles that fill our days, and the remarkable nature of a cosmic wisdom that seems to lead the way. One's life becomes very full when the calendar is taken seriously.

And this is just the beginning.

The calendar adds yet other dimensions to the contemplative life style. Each week of the year is associated with different possibilities for immersion in studies. The Talmud can be learned on a daily basis in which a particular page is studied each day by every talmudic student in the world. This is called *daf yomi*, literally meaning the page of the day. Everyone doing this practice is connected on an esoteric plane with like-minded students studying the same material everywhere. Those partaking in daf yomi study complete one cycle of the Talmud every seven years.

Other students break up basic source books in Judaism, like the oral tradition known as the *Mishna*, and memorize parts according to a schedule. Some memorize psalms. Some study particular books. One of the best known of these is the *Tanya*, by Shneur Zalman of Lyady, the founder of Habad Hasidism, which is outlined for daily study according to the calendar. In this way, one assures cycling through the text on a regular basis year after year.

The most far reaching study in the Jewish world is the weekly selection of the Torah, the Five Books of Moses, which is divided into an annual cycle that begins each year on Simcha Torah (The Joy of Torah), at the end of Sukkot. The weekly portion is the same for Jewish students around the world, every week of the year. This weekly study of Torah portions links up the worldwide Jewish community on a number of levels and carries with it a special power of connectedness, for no matter where one is studying, even in a cabin deep in the woods, there is a knowing on a subtle level that the same words are being repeated and learned in various parts of the world.

Sabbaths are identified by the Torah portion being read that day. The energy of the readings permeates the day and affects the teachings and, in many ways, the mood of the day. In addition, many Sabbaths are identified by upcoming events, which also significantly impact on the experience of the day. Here is a list of special Sabbaths:

- *Shabbat Mevarkhin* (Blessing Sabbath): The dozen Sabbaths each year immediately preceding the new moon, whose date is announced publicly to the congregation during the prayer services. A time of "out with the old, in with the new."
- *Shabbat Rosh Hodesh* (New Moon Sabbath): When a Shabbat coincidentally falls on a new moon day, requiring special prayers. A time of connecting with the moon cycles.
- *Shabbat Shuvah* (Returning Sabbath): The Sabbath day that falls during the Ten Days of Awe between Rosh Hashana and Yom Kippur. Requires a change in some prayers. A time of repentance.
- *Shabbat Hol ha-Mo'ed* (Festival Day Sabbath): Falls during the weeks of Passover and Sukkot. Requires special prayers. In addition, Song of Songs is read during Passover and *Ecclesiastics* is read during Sukkot. A special time related to the Passover (freedom) or Sukkot (gratitude).

- *Shabbat Chanukkah:* Occurs once or twice during Chanukkah. Additional prayer readings are read at this time. This may coincide with Rosh Hodesh. A time of special awareness of the infinite light (Ohr Ein Sof).
- *Shabbat Shirah* (Song Sabbath): The Sabbath coinciding with the Torah reading of the song at the crossing of the Red Sea in Exodus 15. A time of appreciation for miracles, big and small.
- *Shabbat Shakelim* (Shekel Sabbath): Occurs on the Shabbat immediately preceding the Hebrew month of *Adar,* which contains Purim. Special Torah readings required related to the giving by each adult of half a shekel. A time of giving special tzeddakah (contributions).
- *Shabbat Zakhor* (Remembrance Sabbath): The Sabbath preceding Purim. Special readings are offered regarding potential destruction. A time to reflect on fate.
- *Shabbat Parah* (Red Heifer Sabbath): The two Sabbaths preceding the first of the Hebrew month of *Nisan,* or the Sabbath preceding the first of Nisan if it itself is a Sabbath. Special readings on the ritual purification of the ashes of the red heifer, an esoteric rite of purification (Numbers 19:1–22). Reflection on the meaning of spiritual defilement.
- *Shabbat ha-Hodesh* (Sabbath of the Beginning): The Sabbath preceding the first of Nisan, or the first of Nisan itself if it falls on a Sabbath. Although Rosh Hashana is viewed as the New Year, occuring on the first of *Tishrey,* this is actually considered as the seventh Hebrew month. The first month is officially Nisan, which includes Passover. Special reading of the details and ritual laws of Passover. A time to reflect on being trapped and what it takes to achieve freedom. On an esoteric level, it is also a time to reflect on beginnings and endings of cycles.
- *Shabbat Ha-Gadol* (Great Sabbath): The Sabbath preceding Passover. A time of psychological preparation and study of the elements of the upcoming seder.
- *Shabbat Hazon* (Sabbath of Vision): The Sabbath preceding Tisha b'Av (the ninth of Av). Special readings of punishment. Lamentations is read. A time of deep reflection

of reward and punishment. Occurs during the first nine days of Av, a mourning period with restrictions on cutting hair, shaving, washing clothes, and dressing.

• *Shabbat Nahamu* (Sabbath of Comforting): The Sabbath immediately following Tisha b'Av, with special readings from Isa 40:1. As Tisha b'Av is a strict fast and day of mourning, this is a time of relief and letting go. A time to experience being held in the arms of the Divine.

History of the Sabbath

The Sabbath is first mentioned early in the Torah, in the opening paragraph of the second chapter of Genesis, which refers to God "resting" after the "work" of Creation. Thus, as we are viewed as God-like creatures, having been created in the image of God, we are obliged to follow this lead to rest on the seventh day. Each Friday night this verse is read as part of the sanctification of the wine or grape juice *(kiddush)* that marks the opening of the first celebratory meal of the Sabbath.

We learn more about the uniqueness of this day when the Israelites are surviving on *manna* collected in the desert. As the manna would last for only one day before rotting—*it bred worms and stank* (Exodus 16:20)—the daily collection had to be consumed immediately. However, on the day before the Sabbath, the people were instructed to collect a double portion, so as not to have to work to collect food on the Sabbath. This turned out well because on the Sabbath the manna *neither stank nor had worms* (Exodus 16:24). This leads to the mystical conclusion that the Sabbath is not an ordinary day. We could go so far as to say it is a phenomenon out of time and space. There are six days, and there is the Sabbath, which is not a day but a kind of timeless, spaceless phenomenon.

Herein also lies the secret of the teaching of abundance vis-à-vis the Sabbath. Many people feel that they cannot afford to stop all of their worldly activities on this day. But the teachings say that there will not be a price to pay for taking the time off; rather it can only help in the sense that we will be spiritually refreshed. This is something we can only discover through direct experience by seeing what happens when we actually do it.

As we will see, there are two types of Sabbath retreat we can undertake: family retreats and solo retreats. Either way— spending quality time with our loved ones, or communing one-on-one with nature and God—it is a win-win situation.

In the writings of prophets Jeremiah and Ezekiel, the fate of Jerusalem is often connected with the observance or desecration of the Sabbath. The literal meaning of Jerusalem is "City of Peace." The mystical understanding of these teachings is that our inner Jerusalem, the place of inner peace, depends upon being nurtured spiritually—and this is what the Sabbath is about. All the way back to the Maccabean revolt, Jews have often chosen death over desecrating the Sabbath (1 Macc 2:31–38). This could be viewed as straight martyrdom over beliefs, or, on a deeper level, it could be seen as a profound realization that the Sab-bath is the vehicle for understanding the whole purpose of life; without it, there is no reason to live.

The Sabbath is by Jewish law a time of joy. Mourning a death is not permitted on the Sabbath, even for a close family member. It is a time to honor our parents. One cannot fast, but must celebrate with the best food and drink. Three good meals are mandated. It is a day when we wear our best clothes. It is also considered meritorious to have sexual relations with one's spouse on the Sabbath.

We are taught that if one Sabbath was observed by everyone, it would assure the immediate appearance of messianic consciousness. It is said also that keeping the Sabbath alone is equal to observing the entire collection of Jewish law. The experience of the Sabbath is viewed as a taste of the "world-to-come." This is considered an opportunity for an ordinary person to enjoy a connection with life that even the greatest kings and monarchs of all times sought to achieve, a connection that is

available not through wealth and power but through simply
learning how to stop being busy.

The Sabbath as a Day of Retreat

As this is a handbook for meditation practice, it is important to
distinguish between meditation, per se, and meditation retreats.
As previously noted, meditation is an umbrella term that
includes many techniques designed to alter consciousness.
Some of these methods are quite brief, lasting only a few
minutes; some can continue for a long time. Meditation retreats
are extended periods of time that are given exclusively to
meditation practices for the purpose of transformation and
expanding one's consciousness. Retreats can include as few as
only one or two meditation practices, repeated over and over
again, or retreats can consist of a collection of different
meditative techniques. Whatever combination of practices we
use, however, retreats are defined by the amount of consecutive
time one is able to devote to meditation practice.

Many people meditate for twenty to sixty minutes on a daily
basis. This is an excellent way to sustain a level of meditative
consciousness. But when we wish to transform ourselves and
deepen our awareness, we must shift away from our normal life
style long enough to allow our inner chemistry to change.
Traditionally, this can be accomplished by retreating into a
concentrated meditative environment for at least a day or more
at a time. We can arbitrarily distinguish between ordinary
meditation and a designated retreat by setting a standard of a
minimum of twelve hours of continuous practice.

Judaism literally mandates one full twenty-four hour day
of retreat—a Sabbath day—every week of an adult's life. It
also mandates week-long retreats in the spring and fall. For
highly committed practitioners, Judaism has opportunities
for extended retreats of between thirty and forty-nine days a
couple of times a year.

Retreats of this length are common in many contemplative traditions. Vajrayana Buddhists often take retreats

of thirty days; Theravada Buddhists traditionally take a three-month retreat every year. To become a lama in some Tibetan practices, one must sit on retreat consecutively for three years, three months, and three days.

Clearly, extended retreats are not for everyone. Moreover, they are not necessary in order to become a highly skilled meditation practitioner. The point here is that traditional Judaism for thousands of years up to this very day has followed a program of practice that requires at least one full day of retreat every week plus two weeks of retreat every year. This applies to people with busy lives, and is a commitment that serious meditators must consider.

We are never more than six days away from the one-day retreat possibility intrinsic in every Shabbat. We have seen here that about one-half of all Shabbats have special designations that add new elements to a retreat taken at that time. In addition, almost every month has a unique minor or major holy day that gives opportunities for retreats of several days or more. When we include all of the designated possibilities for Jewish-oriented retreat days, it turns out to be about 140 days each year!

This opportunity each of us has to experience time off, to commune with nature, and to be at one with the Divine, is an amazing gift. The Talmud teaches, "The Holy One said to Moses: Moses, I have a precious gift in my treasury and its name is Shabbat and I wish to give it..." (*Beitzah* 16a) We have the choice to accept this gift, or not.

It is taught that our willingness and desire to dwell continuously in the arms of the Divine and to fully immerse in the truth of oneness is the key to all of the wisdom of this universe. This can be achieved by simply letting go, by regularly practicing—at least one full day each week—reflection, silence, simplicity, and other meditative techniques discussed in this book. It is a transformative experience to take advantage of this gift, and it is more important than all the riches of the world. For this reason, it is said, "Judaism does not keep Shabbat alive as much as Shabbat keeps Judaism alive."

Solo Retreats

Five things have included in them one-sixtieth part of something else. They are fire, honey, Shabbat, sleep, and dreams. Fire has one-sixtieth of hell; honey has one-sixtieth of manna; Shabbat has one-sixtieth of heaven; sleep has one-sixtieth of death; and dreams have one-sixtieth of prophecy.

Babylonian Talmud: *Berachot* 57b

A day of spiritual retreat is a powerful vehicle for renewing the soul. Many people, however, are unfamiliar with the broad selection of spiritual practices outlined in this book. Thus, when we find a way to take a day to ourselves, we often do not know what to do with the free time.

The purpose of a spiritual retreat is to do things that are different, to engage in experiences that will change our perspective of life and our role in it. Initially, these practices are not the kinds of things we would normally choose to do during our free time. Some require strong concentration, some are repetitive, some necessitate great patience. On the other hand, many spiritual practices are intriguing, stimulating, provocative, and transformative. Although the introduction to spiritual practice is often an unusual experience, many of us discover that something within us opens, we gain new access to an inner voice, and we find ourselves looking forward to repeating and reinforcing the experience.

If you have never taken a day off for spiritual practice, you have a treat in store. This chapter will describe the things one needs to consider when planning a solo retreat.* Before planning your day of retreat, you need to first experience a variety of the exercises in Basic Jewish Meditation Practices, described in the first section of this book. With this experience under your belt, you can select one or more practices that you would like to begin to perfect. These will be the practices of your retreat.

Set up a gentle schedule for yourself, following one of the recommended timetables you will find in the appendix. Be careful not to make the schedule too rigorous for your first day of retreat experience. Give yourself plenty of time to rest during the day. Start only with practices that are most meaningful for you, the ones that seem to work the best to capture your attention and quiet your mind. Set up a couple of different sample days to consider and then begin to make your plans for a day off. You will decide on which schedule to follow just before you begin the actual day of your retreat, after experiencing many different exercises.

Timing

How do we find time to take a day for a retreat? This is a question most people ask themselves. Our busy lives often impose tight scheduling. We allow ourselves a certain amount of time to get from one place to another, and often become extremely agitated if a traffic jam ruins the schedule. We have a fixed amount of time for work or projects, and frequently run overtime. We are constantly pressured to assure time for our most intimate relationships with family members. We even find ourselves cutting into our basic time requirements for life

*For greater detail on planning a retreat in your own home, see my book *Silence, Simplicity & Solitude* (SkyLight Paths Publishing, 1999).

essentials such as eating and sleeping. At certain periods, the demands of time seem to carry us surfing on a giant wave, desperately trying to keep our balance. Thus, given the level of our daily activity, who has time for spiritual retreat?

On the other hand, when we come down with a minor illness, we may have to stop everything for a few days, stay in bed, and nurse ourselves back to health. Remarkably, the world goes on without us. We may be missed, but the family gets fed, the important daily activities are put on hold, and life continues. So the issue is not as much about time as it is about how we prioritize our lives.

When we are caught in the hectic flow of daily life, our sense of priority is often confused. Things become clearer when we face a crisis. When, God forbid, someone in the family has a serious accident or faces a life-threatening illness, we suddenly gain clarity about our priorities. When a person is given only months to live, he or she instantly realizes that, in the end, time is the most valuable commodity we have.

Planning Time Off

Stop for a moment and reflect on your life up to now. It is sometimes useful in this reflection to imagine that you have just come from the doctor's office, and she has told you (may this never happen!) that you have only a few months to live. Please think about how you have lived your life until now and how you would change it if you could.

Perhaps everything has been perfect for you and you would not change a thing. You have lived a blessed life. Most people discover in this type of reflection, however, that they would focus more on quality time if they had it to do over. Quality time includes opportunities for better connections in relationships and more quiet, unengaged personal time for reflection and contemplation.

Obviously, we can do nothing about the past. The question is: Do you want to bring more quality time into the future? Would you like to take a few days every so often and just be with yourself? How would you like to take off one day each week and do nothing but read, meditate, and engage in spiritual practices?

The idea of setting aside one day a week is mind-boggling for many of us, but it is important to note that hundreds of thousands of traditional Jews do in fact celebrate Shabbat every week without fail. A large percentage of these practitioners are engaged in highly active lives—running successful businesses, often involved in professional occupations—and yet they would never entertain the thought of working on Shabbat. It is simply a matter of priorities.

Thus, taking off a day or two for personal spiritual practice is not really as difficult as it sounds. The real challenge is what we choose to do with the time.

There is an essential difference between taking a vacation and using precious free time for spiritual renewal. In my book, *A Heart of Stillness,* I describe the four fundamental elements that differentiate simple relaxation from spiritual practice: (1) *purification,* which involves separating from the mundane world; (2) *concentration,* which helps to focus and clarify the mind; (3) *effort,* which is the outward expression of willpower; and (4) *mastery,* which is the discipline needed to succeed.

Because your retreat needs to be designed for spiritual renewal rather than relaxation, there are a number of points to consider. In essence, you will need to provide a sanctuary for yourself that will not be violated except in an emergency.

Location

Many people are able to retreat in their own homes. Obviously, this is easier if we live alone or with only one other adult in the household. When other people are involved, a person interested in taking a retreat at home must be able to designate a "sacred space" that can be closed off from the rest of the household. If it is not possible to set aside a dedicated sanctuary in your home, then you will need to find another place where you will be safe and secure for the period of your retreat.

A sacred space need not be very large—an eight-by-ten room or cabin is more than enough. It needs to be just large enough for a comfortable sitting arrangement, and big enough for a bed, even if it is merely a foam mat on the floor that can be kept rolled in a corner. In rustic conditions, the sanctuary may have only a hot plate for cooking and a small larder for food items.

If you stay in your own home, the accommodations are most likely luxurious compared with a tiny cabin in the woods. But one of the characteristics of a retreat is that we try to change our normal living arrangements. Thus, even in your home, you may wish to change your bed and bedding, the type of food you eat, or your bathing routine in order to gain a new perspective on habitual behavior patterns.

The most important aspect of the retreat location, however, is that we assure the opportunity of giving our undivided attention to the exercises we wish to undertake. This means that it should be without a telephone, television, radio, or other potentially invasive appliances (fax machine, computer, beeper, and so on).

We may need to put a sign on the door cautioning uninvited visitors not to disturb the people inside—just as we do when there is a newborn baby in the house. Telephones need to be adjusted so that they do not ring and answering machines turned down so that we do not hear the voices. Preferably, all these events take place in another part of the house so that we do not have to be wondering about every call that comes through.

Yet, with all this, it is important to prepare for any emergencies that may arise. When on retreat, we are often concerned about family and friends. It is useful, therefore, for retreats that last three days or longer, to arrange for someone to check the mail and the answering machine each day. In this way, the retreatant will be assured that should an emergency arise, he or she will be quickly notified.

If you are going to a secluded location for your retreat, it is a good idea to let someone know where you are planning to go, how long you will be there, and the best way to contact you if the need arises. This not only relieves any concerns about emergencies but it also provides a security measure in case you get lost in the woods or for some other reason are unable to return home at the appointed time. If that happens, your "guardian" should take steps to verify that you are not in trouble.

All these measures are designed to relieve the retreatant of potential concerns. When we are not following our normal daily routine, we tend to worry, become afraid, and obsess about anything. The more preventative steps we can take while preparing for our retreat, the more opportunity we will have to devote ourselves entirely to the retreat practice.

Family and Friends

Many people take family retreats together (see following section). But if you are planning to do a solo retreat, it is most important to work in advance with family and friends. Although most people love the idea of taking time off for themselves, they tend to worry about others who do the same thing. Thus, family and friends need to be informed of your intentions well in advance.

This is particularly significant, of course, for people living in the same household. A retreatant needs an implicit or explicit "contract" to gain the cooperation of household members during the retreat. This agreement should contain elements that clarify what kind of personal contact is acceptable (minimal or none at all is recommended), how the kitchen will be managed (total independence is desirable), and use of potentially disturbing electronics such as the television (try to assure as much silence as possible). In essence, the rest of the household will be participating in the retreat on one level or another. (Indeed, many retreatants soon discover that they are not the only ones benefiting from their retreat!)

When friends are informed in advance, telephone calls and casual visits are minimized. It is hoped that friends will be curious and supportive; this will encourage the retreatant and help to build confidence. The primary purpose of preparing family and friends is, once again, to minimize the potential for disruption of the retreat and to ease one's mind.

It is important to note here that traditional Jewish families celebrate Shabbat as a communal experience. Everyone in the household participates, building a supportive environment, and this is enormously beneficial for setting the tone of the day. That is why there is a separate section of this book on family retreats. When possible, I highly recommend family cooperation in this process.

However, as many people begin spiritual practice independently, this book is also designed for individuals embarking on their own. Either way, whether on Shabbat or other days, whether in a group situation, a family, or alone, the celebration of the spirit is an important part of nurturing our souls. While we invest an enormous amount of time in meeting our food needs for the body, we must pay increasing attention in these busy times to feeding the soul.

Food for the Body

Most people do not realize how much food-related time is spent in daily life. We read about food, think about it, talk about it, dream about it. We spend time getting to the market, shopping, reading the labels, traveling to different stores for various items, preparing, cooking, setting the table, eating, and cleaning up after ourselves. In between, we are often drinking tea or coffee, snacking, and, of course, thinking about that great restaurant we just visited or intend to visit in the near future.

It is probably conservative to estimate that at least one-third of our waking hours are in some way related to food. When we can minimize the role of food, an enormous amount of free time becomes available to nuture the soul.

Thus, an important aspect of preparing for a retreat is arranging for simple, quick, easy-to-digest meals.

Preparation is the key. My own method is to cook a large vegetable stew or soup that can be heated in minutes, and to make a large mixed salad, which will stay fresh for days when kept in an airtight plastic bag. Breakfast cereal, hot or cold, is easy to prepare and can be eaten anytime during the day. A supply of dried fruits and nuts is always a treat. Advance preparation minimizes the time we spend on food—everything is ready almost instantly, the meals are nutritious, and clean up is simple.

If there are other people in the retreat area, try to minimize or eliminate trips to the kitchen in order to avoid contact. Every contact is a distraction, and often these distractions can hamper one's concentration or even spoil a retreat. The less we encounter other people while doing our inner work, the better. Often, to eliminate casual encounters, it is best to keep a food supply in the place where you are doing your meditation exercises.

If you wish to celebrate Shabbat in the traditional manner, you should be prepared not to cook at any time from sundown Friday until sundown Saturday. In most traditional households, an electric urn is used to keep water hot all day for the preparation of coffee, tea, or instant soup. In addition, an electric hot plate is on all day to keep food warm. Sometimes an electric cooking pot is used to keep a ready supply of hot soup or stew. Sometimes a gas stove or oven turned low is left on all day. Of course, one can eat cold, precooked food at any time.

The basic principles from a traditional perspective are that one should not turn electricity on or off during Shabbat, a fire should not be ignited or extinguished, and food should not be transformed through the cooking process. There are many ways to explain the Shabbat laws, and the truth is that most Jews do not observe these strict laws. Purely from the perspective of spiritual renewal, however, anything we can do to minimize our mundane activities is beneficial—and most of the Shabbat laws do in fact inhibit our regular weekday routine.

Whereas observant Jews eliminate cooking on Shabbat, traditionally the Shabbat meals are festive and filled with special taste treats. Thus, this is the time to splurge, to include your favorite foods and sweets, to fully enjoy the pleasure of eating. Indeed, Jews love food; the archetypal Jewish mother is always associated with chicken soup, gefilte fish, and other goodies that were invariably served on Shabbat or the holy days. Except for Yom Kippur and Tisha b'Av, which are days of fasting, all the special days of the year are marked by festive meals. One might even say that Jewish social life is inextricably connected with the dinner table.

In preparing your food, move deliberately. Enjoy the feel, look, and smell of the food. Handle it with love. Imagine how you would be relating to this food if you were just coming out of a wasteland where there was nothing to eat. In other words, experience the food in a special way, with caring, respect, and deep appreciation. The point is that although eating food serves a primary purpose, the preparation itself can be a marvelous spiritual practice that will enhance your state of mind and greatly benefit the overall retreat experience.

Willpower and Determination

The secret ingredient for success in all retreats—and in all of life for that matter—is preparing ourselves to see the task through. A halfhearted approach will not yield the strength of conviction we need to bring our unruly minds under control. We must always remember that while the mind is a wonderful organ, allowing us to do things unequaled in the rest of nature, we must not permit our minds to dominate us. The most insidious idol worship of all is the belief that the mind is supreme.

Many people misinterpret Descartes's famous dictum, "I think, therefore I am." In his philosophy, the sense of our existence, our knowing that we are something or somebody, is dependent upon our minds. But it is mistaken to believe that existence *itself* is contingent upon our minds. A tree does not have cognitive abilities, but it is still a tree. We would not be the same without our ability to think, but our existence is not conditional upon this ability.

One of the main tasks of spiritual inquiry, and one of the primary benefits of meditation, is to appreciate fully, to the greatest extent possible, the what, who, and why of our existence. We are much bigger than our minds—we have mysterious qualities, energies, and forces operating within each of us. Our yearning to discover the truth of our existence, the very motivation that has you reading these words at this moment, is centered in an unknown spark that transcends the mind. Thus, it is only when we grasp the inner workings of our minds that we can achieve a deeper wisdom.

One of the most important tools for understanding the mind is gained through deepening insight into our power of will. The will is a much more elementary human attribute than the mind. Although the mind may be running rampant, we can will ourselves to sit still. Although the mind may demand incessantly that we do something, we can will ourselves to do nothing. The mind is a powerful engine, but the will sits in the driver's seat.

Many people do not realize that the will is ultimately in control. The will is often hidden in the shadows: We act on impulse or find ourselves propelled by emotions. Perhaps the most common mind state is one that "wants" something, either to avoid discomfort or to accommodate every desire that arises. But of course we cannot satisfy all our desires, nor can we avoid discomfort in life.

As long as we believe that we are our minds, we are continually dissatisfied, constantly "wanting" something. Once we appreciate the deeper level of the will, that it can check and neutralize desire, we enter into a new relationship with our thought processes and we gain the potential to become truly liberated.

We all exercise our wills in the flow of life, but the process of meditation and inner work is a unique challenge for developing the power of will. We are not attempting to accomplish a task or achieve a goal; rather, we are focused on understanding our own makeup, what makes us tick. Thus, everything in meditative practice becomes grist for the mill.

In the meditation process, when we like something, we notice that we like it. When we want to avoid doing something, we notice how this desire for avoidance affects us. But rather than acting on our thoughts or feelings, we simply notice. This noticing without acting is dependent upon the will, and the more we are able to constrain our actions, the more we develop our power of will.

For our retreat to be successful, we need in the beginning to have the determination to see it through, to do the exercises and follow the instructions. Many times throughout the retreat we will find that we want to do something else. Invariably, it will be something that would take us back to our normal pattern—read a book or magazine, watch television, raid the refrigerator, sleep away the afternoon. This is something to notice, but by staying with the task we build the power of will.

The more we appreciate that our wills really can be in control, the quieter our minds become. And this is what the retreat is about. The quieter the mind, the more deeply we are able to see into things. From this, we realize that we are in a much different world. It is a world of natural harmony, profound wisdom, and sensual delight. It is here, right now, if only we break through the veils of our own minds.

Learn about and befriend the will. It is our greatest asset in spiritual inquiry, the bedrock upon which true awareness can be cultivated.

Retreats of Three Days or Longer

A three-day retreat provides a good amount of time to enter deeply into the environment of silence. Many changes can occur in this period. Thus, a spiritual retreat from Friday morning to Sunday night is highly recommended.

Outside the land of Israel, many Jewish holy days are celebrated for forty-eight rather than twenty-four hours. The main celebrations of Passover, Shavuot, and Sukkot extend for several days, so these are good times to undertake longer retreats.

The diverse spiritual exercises described in this handbook are sufficient for you to design a retreat of any length. As noted earlier, just the basic practices of sitting and walking meditation are the primary exercises for many retreats that extend for weeks or months. The point is not to keep trying new practices, but to find those that work best and then to master them through constant repetition.

In the appendix to this handbook, there are a number of suggested meditative programs for day-long—or longer— retreats. These are examples of custom-designed personal retreats that selectively utilize the exercises in this book for specific goals. This allows a retreatant great flexibility to follow one of these schedules or to custom design a schedule for himself or herself.

Solo retreats are crucial for spiritual transformation. Once people are familiar with the experience of one day off a week on a regular basis, they usually view it as absolutely the minimum requirement for living a meaningful spiritual life. Great spiritual leaders in almost all traditions made profound discoveries while on retreat. Moreover, most people who are able to take week-long or longer retreats invariably point to these experiences as among the most important of their lives. This time on personal retreat provides a springboard that helps meditators achieve new levels of practice.

A large number of dedicated long-term retreatants are middle-aged or older. Working with inner silence is a superb practice for preparing ourselves for the later years of life, when there can be considerable time for quiet and being alone. It is also an excellent practice to appreciate what life is about as we come face-to-face with our own mortality.

Younger people, particularly when engaged in active family life, usually do not have the time or inclination to do many extended solo retreats. The family itself is the center of one's spiritual life. Judaism as a spiritual tradition is particularly family oriented. This is seen most clearly in group participation and celebration of Shabbat and holy days. The following section explores the contemplative possibilities for bringing families together for true quality time every week. This section on family retreats should be read by anyone interested in the experience of meditative awareness when celebrating Shabbat, whether alone or with a group.

Family Retreats

Rabbi Yossi the son of Rabbi Yehuda said: "Two ministering angels escort a person on Sabbath eve from the house of prayer to his or her home. One is an angel of good and one is an angel of evil. When the person enters and finds the candles lit, the table set, and the bed in order [everything is prepared for the mood of Shabbat], then the angel of good says, 'May the next Shabbat be like this one.' And the angel of evil [must] answer 'Amen' [thus seconding the good angel's blessing]. However, if the house is not arranged for Shabbat [and nothing is changed from the mood of the weekdays], then the angel of evil says, 'May the next Shabbat be like this one,' and the angel of good must say, 'Amen.'"

Babylonian Talmud: *Shabbat* 119b

Traditional Jews observe a strict set of laws regarding Shabbat, all of which minimize activity in the ordinary world, thereby allowing the practitioner to devote almost all of his or her time to spiritual experiences. As these laws include restrictions on handling money, watching television, answering telephones, using computers, cooking, travel, and so on, entire families are able to share a special time together in an undistracted environment dedicated to prayer, study, family and community relations, and simply being.

As this experience of quality time is the norm in traditional Jewish households, children accept this as a way of life from the beginning. This acceptance is further enhanced when all of the friends of the family and their respective children also observe the Sabbath in similar ways. Most nontraditional Jewish families are not in this situation. Observance of the Sabbath is not a way of life for them or most of their friends. Yet, it is possible to begin to get the flavor of quality time for the family by setting some guidelines and by exploring some of the nuances of the basic Sabbath rituals.

The guidelines for a family Shabbat experience obviously will have to be custom-designed by each family, depending upon the needs of the individual members. At the beginning, there needs to be some understanding and a level of agreement, on what it means to take time off for quiet and reflection. There needs to be a certain amount of willingness to experiment as well as a commitment to revisit the issues in family meetings on a fairly frequent basis. The ultimate goal is to refresh the souls of the individual family members and the family soul itself.

The process of working with these questions is beneficial. Many families do not even take the time to talk about these things. Once the discussion is opened, there are often widely divergent ideas expressed. This can be a challenging undertaking. Sometimes everyone will agree to work together, other times they will agree to give each person enough freedom to do the Sabbath in his or her own way. In any case, with mutual respect and a sincere desire to attain a new quality of life, progress will be accomplished.

At the very least, it is hoped that the family would agree to spend festive meal times together, which is the time when many Sabbath rituals are observed. This alone gives a flavor that many people keep in their hearts as a warm and loving experience. For some people, their sole connection with the Sabbath as a child is related to a grandmother lighting candles on Friday night. This can be profoundly moving and is just a hint of the possibility of bringing some aspects of the Sabbath into modern family life.

The subjects that the family could address include the following:

What kind of shared activities lend themselves to quality time with one another?

What subjects of study would people be willing to mutually undertake to provide for stimulating and inspirational conversation and sharing?

To what degree are individual family members willing to give up some of their normal activities to spend more time with the family?

Is there any interest in joining with a larger community that celebrates the Sabbath, either in community centers or at prayer services?

Is there any interest in exploring different meditative techniques—as described in this book—as a way for the family to be together?

Is there willingness to make a commitment to a certain number of hours each Sabbath day, or a fixed number of Sabbaths each month, that everyone will agree to, no matter what comes up?

Will people participate in the food purchasing, preparation, service, and clean up so that the strain of the festive meals can be shared by all?

Are individuals willing to undertake learning and guiding rituals, both those that follow in this chapter, as well as rituals custom-designed by the family itself?

These are general subjects for family discussion. The direction of the discussion will quickly take its own course. Now let us take a look at contemplative approaches to the Sabbath ritual that can be done either by individuals or families as a whole. These rituals can be the foundation upon which the family explores other possibilities to deepen the Sabbath experience and to turn the day into a family retreat.

Kavannah in Preparing for Shabbat (or a Holy Day)

Preparation for a Shabbat will have considerable influence on the experience of the day. Just as with any retreat, we must prepare in advance for our physical, emotional, and intellectual needs so that our spiritual well-being can be properly attended. Maintaining strong kavannah and continuity awareness is crucial during the Shabbat preparation time.

In traditional Jewish homes, preparation for the Friday evening festive meal of Shabbat often begins as early as Wednesday. Food purchases, cooking, and cleaning are all part of the process. Be sure to give yourself enough time to get the things you will need. And prepare as much in advance as possible so that you do not have to become involved in too many details while you are doing your meditative practice.

It is well known that tensions often run high in traditional Jewish homes on Friday afternoon as preparations for Shabbat reach maximum intensity. This can lead to regrettable emotional flare-ups, and it often leaves a residue that carries into Shabbat. People are emotionally drained, exhausted when Shabbat arrives, and this clearly is not the way you will be able to accomplish much in renewing your soul. Thus, pay close attention to your preparations. The best way to do this is to make the preparation a spiritual practice in itself, to bring your kavannah, your continuity practice, your higher awareness, to every aspect of the preparation.

PHYSICAL PREPARATION

Prepare your body. It is customary to bathe before Shabbat or a holy day. (As noted earlier, many observant Jews visit the mikveh in preparation for Shabbat.) This bathing need not be as extensive as the ablutions that were described earlier, but it should be done in the same spirit. Wash yourself meditatively, dry yourself consciously, experience the fullness of your physical being. Prepare yourself meticulously as if you were about to attend the most important event of your life. Pampering your physical being brings you into greater intimacy with your soul. Renewing the body is an important ingredient for renewing the soul.

The house should be prepared for the Sabbath as one would prepare a house for welcoming the most honored guests. Often a white table cloth is set, the best dishes and silverware are used, the table is set with the ritual utensils—candleholders, kiddush cup, a bottle of wine or grape juice, challah (if you have it) under a decorative cover. A nice standard in traditional Jewish homes is for a husband to give his wife flowers for Shabbat each week. Think about giving something to a family member. Set the scene each week for the specialness it deserves.

Dress in festive clothes. People often wear white on Shabbat; kabbalists dress completely in white. Imagine that you have a date with your highest soul and want to be in a relaxed, comfortable, balanced state of mind. Try to time yourself so that you are completely dressed and all food is ready 45 minutes before the time of sunset (listed in the daily newspaper, or on a Jewish calendar). Now you are ready for candle lighting and the basic rituals of the Sabbath.

MEDITATIVE CANDLE LIGHTING

(45 minutes; begin 30 minutes before the official time of sunset)

**Just as the light of a candle remains
undiminished even if it is the source for a million
candles to be kindled, so will the fulfillment of a
good deed not cause a person to suffer any
decrease of his or her essential wealth.**

Exodus Rabbah 36:3

In Judaism, the turn of the day is sunset rather than midnight. (In ancient times before clocks, sunset and sunrise were clear to everyone, while midnight was difficult to determine and could only be vaguely approximated.) As we enter into the "day" of Shabbat or any holy day, just before sunset, candles are always lighted in traditional households. The lighting of candles is the pivotal point when we let go of the activities and thoughts of daily living and enter into the atmosphere and equilibrium of *menucha*, the rest of spiritual renewal.

Candle lighting is always a wonderful experience. It was, and still is, a timeless moment, a pause and reflection upon life's purpose, and most important, a time of thanksgiving for the health and well-being of the family.

Prepare now to light candles.

1. Preferably choose candles that are approximately three to four inches long and three-fourths of an inch in diameter. In many supermarkets you can purchase standard Shabbat candles that burn 3 to 4 hours. Most households light two candles every Sabbath; some burn an extra candle for each child in the family.

2. Be sure to use candleholders that will not be harmed when the candles burn all the way down, and that are not dangerous if left unattended. Traditionally, once Shabbat has begun, we allow all flames to extinguish themselves and

never blow them out unless there is a danger of starting a life-threatening fire.

3. Once your candles are set in their holders and just before lighting them, the family should stop and sit for 5 or 10 minutes, reflecting upon the past week, trying to let go of anything that is pressing or demanding attention. People may wish to write themselves notes at this time, a reminder to attend to something after the Sabbath so that there is no need to worry about it. Do not spend too long because you will be sitting and meditating again after lighting the candles—the candles should be lighted before dark.

4. Spend a couple of minutes looking outside, watching the fading light, experiencing the impending nightfall.

5. Now it is time to light. Candle lighting should be done approximately 20 minutes before sundown. With awareness, experience your movements and the sensual experience of striking a match and lighting the candles.

6. From a kabbalistic perspective, the candle on the right represents *chesed,* the lovingkindness of creation, all the gifts we have: our health, our relationships, our financial well-being, our minds, food on our table, our ability to love and be loved. The candle on the left represents *gevorah,* cosmic justice, the karmic implications of all our thoughts, words, and actions as well as the thoughts, words, and actions of those around us.

7. After lighting the candles, have everyone sweep their arms three times as if gathering the light of the candles into their heart and soul (some people do this seven times). Everyone should cover their eyes with their hands and think about the chesed and gevorah in their life at this moment. When ready, the leader should offer one of the following blessings.

The traditional Hebrew blessing said just after the ritual lighting of candles is: *Baruch attah Adonoi, Eloheynu melach haolam, asher kidshanu bemitzvotav vitzivanu lahadlick ner shel Shabbat.* (Blessed art thou, Lord, our God, king of the universe, who sanctified us with commandments, and commanded us to light the Sabbath lights.)

The feminine blessing that many people in Jewish Renewal say is: *Barucha at Ya, Shekhina, Ruah ha-olam, asher kidshanu bemitzvotah, vitzivanu lahadlick ner shel Shabbat.* (Blessed is "Ya"—a more neutral word for God—feminine divine presence, spirit of the universe, who sanctified us with her commandments, and commanded us to light the Sabbath lights.)

8. Allow time for each person to say a personal blessing in his or her own words, either openly or silently. This is a time to pray for family and loved ones, expressing whatever gratefulness one may be feeling in this moment of peace and reflection.

9. Now the family should take 5 to 10 minutes in full contemplation. Think about yourself and the immediate family, experience gratitude for what you have, and ask the unknown and unknowable for what you need. This process of asking is, in a strange way, fulfilling. And this time, immediately following candle lighting, is traditionally one of the special times during the week in which we feel most connected with the influx of divine energy.

Traditionally, this is the time when the feminine aspect of God, called the *Shekhina*, makes its presence known, almost palpably. Many special kabbalistic prayers and psalms are said and sung at this time. If you are not familiar with them, sit quietly and imagine that the glow of the candlelight is the caress of the Shekhina as she fills the room with softness and a loving embrace. Thus, Shabbat arrives.

At this point, the family or individuals may wish to take 30–45 extra minutes and do a sitting meditation, as described in the preceding chapter. This is a perfect time to quiet down, reflect, and let go of the events of the past week.

Allow yourselves to drink deeply the nectar of the divine presence, being here in the moment, in the shalom (peace, wholeness) of Shabbat. Enjoy this exceptional time.

MEDITATION PRACTICES FOR SHABBAT DINNER

> Rav Yehuda said: "All who take delight [oneg] in
> the Sabbath will be granted their heart's desires,
> for it says [Psalm 37:4], 'And delight [oneg]
> thyself in the Lord, and It will give you all the
> wishes of your heart.'"
>
> Babylonian Talmud: *Shabbat* 118a

Very few people appreciate the meditative experience of eating. We are almost always doing something else in addition to experiencing our meal. As a result, although we sometimes appreciate our food, we miss most of the sensual, deeply satisfying aspects of nourishing our bodies.

Here is an opportunity to experience the amazing spectrum of taste and olfactory sensations, as well as the physical reactions and mood shifts between mouthfuls of food.

First, before eating, there is a contemplative Shabbat ritual that is worth experiencing. It heightens our awareness, builds anticipation, and awakens our souls. This is the three-fold ritual of kiddush, hand washing, and saying a blessing over the bread.

Kiddush

Kiddush is a blessing of sanctification said over wine (usually sweet, kosher, red wine), or sometimes over grape juice. Kiddush is said on Shabbat and holy days and at weddings, circumcisions, and other joyous or holy events. It is a ritual of remembrance and an invocation. The remembrance is a momentary reminder to be grateful for our freedom and our ability to connect with many layers of reality. The invocation is to call upon our souls and the realms in which they dwell in order to expand this moment of experience into the highest domain of awareness.

1. It is preferable to have a ritual goblet for the kiddush, but any cup or glass will do. It should be sufficient in size to hold enough wine or juice to fill at least one cheekful.

2. Rinse the container and fill it to the brim with wine or juice. Most people stand during this kiddush; some sit. Hold the cup in your right hand and contemplate for 1 or 2 minutes that this ritual has been done hundreds of millions of times throughout history.

3. The Jewish mystical approach to kiddush is that it is a process of harmonizing energies, of sweetening the harshness of life, and of raising the fallen sparks of our awareness to new levels of sanctification. The right hand is chesed (lovingkindness) that holds a vessel containing wine, which represents gevorah (justice/restraint).

Consider the implications of this act of sanctification as if you were able to raise yourself to the highest aspects of creation, to dwell in the angelic realms, to broaden your understanding of life from this perspective.

4. There is a traditional kiddush in Hebrew found in many prayer books. If you are not comfortable with this, let your heart sing a personal song of thankfulness and invocation while you say the simple form of the kiddush, which is very easy to learn: *Baruch attah Adonoi, Elohaynu melach ha-olam, boray pri hagofen.* (Blessed are you, Lord, our God, king of the universe, who created the fruit of the vine.) If you prefer, custom design your own kiddush blessing.

5. Drink the wine or juice thoughtfully, tasting it and enjoying its aroma. This is the entry point and full immersion into the spirit of Shabbat.

Hand Washing

The act of eating is considered not only to be a source of physical nourishment, but also to have mystical connotations.

Food contains energy but no consciousness as we know it. By eating, we convert raw energy and uplift it into a new potential for awareness. This transformative act can be viewed as spiritual alchemy that brings an entirely new perspective to the basic concept of the food chain. Normally, we consider the food chain from a biological viewpoint, leading from simple to complex forms of life. Spiritually, however, the primary consideration is God-consciousness, or total awareness. Thus, eating can be a primitive act, or it can be a highly evolved act in which consciousness is raised to its highest potential.

To clearly distinguish the human capacity for raising consciousness, we add a ritual hand washing before eating that separates us from all other forms of life. This hand washing is not for physical cleanliness—it is not done with soap or detergent. Rather, it is done simply by pouring water over the hands with kavannah, an inner intention to bring a sense of the sacred to the act of eating.

1. Use a cup, glass, or vessel that has a level rim without a spout. Ideally, it should be large enough to hold water to wet both hands from the wrist to the fingertips two times. If the cup is too small, you can refill it as you go.

2. There are a few methods of doing this washing. Some people first pour two quantities over the right hand, enough to get everything wet from the wrist down, and then pour twice over the left hand in the same manner. Others pour right, left, right, left, once each. In the end, the objective is to be sure that each hand has been thoroughly rinsed with water.

3. When pouring water over your hands, imagine that it is washing away spiritual impurities, messy thoughts, hard feelings, unskillful actions, doubts, fears, anger—letting everything go down the drain. Try to empty the mind, become present, enjoy the moment and the feel of the wetness, the sense of purification.

4. Raising the hands, before drying, think of the possibilities of holiness in the act of eating that is about to take place. Quietly consider and pray that the energy derived from the food you are about to eat will be put to the best, highest use as it is transformed into your thoughts, speech, and actions. Pray as well that it will connect your higher consciousness with the Source of all Life.

5. You may wish to say the traditional blessing: *Baruch attah Adonoi, Elohaynu melach ha-olam, asher kidshanu bemitzvotav, vitzivanu al nityalat yadai-im.* (Blessed are you, Lord, our God, king of the universe, who sanctified us with your commandments, and commanded us on the raising up of hands.)

A less traditional blessing (thought or spoken) is:

Thank you, Source of all Being, who leads us in the direction of perfecting ourselves and the universe, and who has guided us to be aware of the awesome act of transmuting energy into higher consciousness by spiritually purifying ourselves in preparation for this act.

6. Dry your hands and return to the table immediately, minimizing distractions, to make a blessing on the bread. The washing of the hands and the blessing of the bread are connected.

7. When doing all of the above in a family group, it is often suggested to have someone else pour water over your hands, and after completing your blessing, to have your hands dried by someone else. This adds a heartwarming dimension to the ritual.

Keep in mind that the washing of hands is in preparation for eating bread. Therefore, *after we finish saying the blessing on the hand washing, everyone remains silent until bread is tasted.* This is a nice quiet time of anticipation. Only the person saying the blessing on the bread speaks, and only to say the blessing itself so that everyone can quickly get a taste of bread.

Ha-Motzi, Blessing the Bread

Bread is considered the primary food source. Traditional Jews always do a hand washing and a blessing when bread is included in any meal, not just on Shabbat. The bread used on Shabbat, however, is different from weekday bread in that a portion of it is taken from the dough before baking to indicate a level of sanctification. The portion taken is called challah, and the bread that results is normally referred to as challah. People often mistake challah for bread that is specially braided or specially sweetened, but challah can look and taste like ordinary bread, except that it is challah because a ritual portion has been taken from the dough.

An easy way to have challah for your festive meal is to buy matzah ahead of time. Be sure that the package indicates that "challah has been taken," which is the case for most of the well-known brands. Matzah does not get stale quickly and is a good substitute when fresh challah is difficult to obtain. If you do not have challah or matzah, however, any bread will do.

It is also a nice idea to bake your own bread for the Sabbath, in which case you can make it challah by following a simple procedure: Just before you are ready to form the dough into loaves, pull off an amount bigger than an olive and smaller than a golf ball. At this point, the traditional blessing is: *Baruch attah Adonoi, Elohaynu melach ha-olam, asher kidshanu bemitzvotav, vitzivanu le-hafrish challah min ha-isah.* (Blessed are you, Lord, our God, king of the universe, who sanctified us with commandments, and commanded us to separate challah from the dough.) The small amount of challah taken is not to be used for anything. Traditionally this dough is burned in a fire, but it is sufficient to wrap it and place it in the trash. Then bake the bread.

The bread should be on the table from the time the table is set, before the kiddush is said. It is usually covered with a cloth, napkin, or specially designed challah cover. There is a hierarchy in the blessings of food, so that if we are presented with three different types of food, say bread, fruit, and vegetables, we say our blessing on the highest level—in this instance, bread. As bread is on a higher level in this hierarchy than wine or juice, we ordinarily would say the blessing on the bread before the kiddush. But for other reasons (determined by the ancient sages), the kiddush comes first; therefore, the bread should be covered, symbolically hidden.

Traditionally, there are two complete loaves, or two whole pieces of matzah. They should not be sliced or broken. They represent the multiple loaves in the ancient temple, and imply that today our home *is* our temple.

Now that it is time to say a blessing on the bread, we pick it up, ideally (from a kabbalistic perspective) touching it with all ten fingers (representing the ten emanations with which the universe was created), and we say a blessing. Everyone touches the bread, or should be linked in some way with someone who is touching the bread, while the blessing is made. In essence, everyone is touching each other or the bread at this wonderful moment.

This, once again, is a good moment to enter into a contemplative mode and consider what was involved in getting this bread or matzah to our meal. Reflect upon preparing the land, planting the wheat seed, tending the sprouts, watering, rain in its season, the nourishment of the sun, the interplay of nature, the ultimate harvest, winnowing, grinding, mixing (taking of challah), baking, packaging, transporting, storing, unpacking, shelving, pricing, and purchasing. At each step, myriad variables branch in all directions, and we soon realize that thousands of people and events were involved in getting this bread to our table. In fact, it is mind-boggling and miraculous that this event has come to pass and that we are about to partake in this food.

This is the kind of contemplation in which we engage as we say the blessing. The traditional blessing is: *Baruch attah Adonoi, Elohaynu melach ha-olam, ha-motzi lechem min ha-aretz.* (Blessed are you, Lord, our God, king of the universe, who brought bread from the earth.)

Here is an open, nontraditional blessing:

Thank you, Mother Nature, who nourishes all living things with your loving sustenance, awesome beauty, and profound wisdom.

Break the bread, dip it in salt (used most of the year, a basic ingredient for survival, and also to remember the tears of life), or in honey (used primarily around the High Holy Days, to change the past and sweeten the moment), and eat a portion slowly, carefully, and contemplatively. Once we have eaten bread, the meal continues without further ritual. In family settings, it is sometimes fun to feed each other a piece of bread. Once the bread is blessed and eaten, we are free to break silence and get to the meal.

Eating the Festive Meal

Normally, the festive meal at Shabbat or on a holy day is an occasion of considerable conversation and interaction. Festive meals are always highlights on the social calendar; they are a time for families and friends to gather and a great time for sharing. However, to the extent that it is possible to avoid ordinary conversation that the family would have at any meal, it is often a much different experience if the discussion centers on a selected subject that is designed to raise spirits and inspire deep inquiry.

In traditional homes, this is often accomplished by talking about the Torah portion of the week. This always provides useful material. However, many other subjects are also appropriate. The object is to avoid mundane conversation as much as possible. This is a time when Hasidic tales are often told, and it is especially a time of singing *niggunim* (see below). In this way, the joy of the day is enhanced and ordinary life is set aside for a while.

For people celebrating alone, or for families that like to experiment, this is also an opportunity to experience the extraordinary richness and joy of eating with deep sensual concentration. Eating meditation follows the same procedure as sitting or walking meditation: We pay close attention to our physical experience in order to heighten awareness of each moment. As with walking, the key to a successful eating meditation is to slow down dramatically so that experiences that normally overlap can be distinguished from one another.

1. Once your food is on the table, look at it for a minute. Smell it, appreciate its texture, color, shape, and consistency.

2. Notice the movements of your hand and arm as you reach for the cutlery. Notice the feel as you pick up the food. Bring the food to your mouth slowly, noticing the experience of anticipation in your mind and in your mouth.

3. Placing the food in your mouth, experience the sensation of warmth or coolness, hardness or softness, crunchiness or smoothness, and discover how the various tastes expand throughout your mouth as you begin to chew.

4. Chew slowly and thoroughly. Notice how you want to reach for the next portion on the plate. Resist this urge until you have swallowed the food in your mouth. Experience the full range of the swallowing.

5. Repeat steps 2–4 over and over again, eating slowly, tasting thoroughly, not taking the next amount until you have swallowed completely.

Throughout this eating meditation, you will probably experience some frustration. We are accustomed to eating much more quickly than this. However, you will also discover an enormous range of taste and texture in your food that you have never before experienced. You will probably discover a sense of fullness and completion after eating less food than usual. In our everyday rush to eat the food on our plates, we bypass the triggers that normally fire when we are satiated. As a result, we eat considerably more food than our bodies need. Meditative eating minimizes this phenomenon. Therefore, take your time, enjoy your food more, eat less, and still feel complete.

Niggunim

A *niggun* is a melody without words that communicates on the level of the soul. It may be a familiar melody, or it may be a spontaneous song that arises from the depths. Many Hasidic rabbis are known by their *niggunim*, their particular way of communicating with the Divine.

It is a common practice to sing Shabbat songs and niggunim at a festive meal. They can be joyous and raucous, but they often have a melodic, contemplative quality. As a meditative practice, singing niggunim is absorbing and transformative. Some people get this from listening to the music. There is usually more value, however, in directly participating, actually making the sound, resonating in the body, reaching into one's heart.

Alone or with family during Shabbat, we are able to set our own rhythms, taking as much time as we wish at each stage. Additionally, we can be less inhibited and can enjoy our own idiosyncrasies. We can also sing completely at ease, expressing the true depths of our inner music.

Therefore, if you know a melody that has a sacred sound, whenever you wish you can stop eating, close your eyes, and sing, hum, or chant this melody as if singing it to a beloved from the depths of your heart. This is a time to feel completely free to compose your own melodies. At first it may be difficult, but try to give yourself permission to make any sounds you wish. Once you feel that you have found a melody line, repeat it over and over again until your entire body is vibrating with the sound. In a family setting, it is fun to listen awhile, and then to join in. Some niggunim are quite well known, others are created on the spot. Be willing to experiment. Have fun.

This practice can lead to blissful and ecstatic states. When we are able to become fully absorbed in the music, we usually discover a new voice, a part within that we have rarely encountered, and this leads us to the contemplation, "Who is singing, and to what is it singing?" Indeed, singing is one of the most universal ways of communing with the Divine—or, as some would say, of the Divine communicating with itself through us.

Grace After Meals

In some traditions, grace is said before eating a meal. In Judaism, the practice is to bless our food before the meal, as we did on the wine and the bread, but to offer grace *after* we have eaten. The traditional Jewish approach is to say or sing a fairly extensive set of prayers. This is done for each meal.

Whether or not you are using these traditional prayers, when the meal is finished, sit quietly for 5 minutes. Someone should be asked to reflect upon the nourishment just experienced, and he or she should express gratitude as fully as possible for all the gifts of life. This sincere affirmation of thankfulness, whether said formally by the book or in one's own words, is the true purpose of the grace after meals. When we are able to connect with the mysterious source of sustenance that continues to keep us alive, we gain higher levels of spiritual awareness.

HAVDALAH MEDITATION

> Rabbi Shimon ben Pazi said: "Whoever sheds tears over the death of a righteous person, the Holy One, blessed be It, stores and numbers [the tears] in the heavenly treasury. As it was said [Psalm 56:9], 'Put my tears into a bottle, and number them.'"
>
> Babylonian Talmud: *Shabbat* 105b

As the sun sets on Saturday evening and stars begin to appear, we prepare to ritualize the separation between the Sabbath just past and the week to come. This is called *havdalah*, the distinction between the sacred and the mundane. Traditionally, havdalah is celebrated with some wine or juice, a candle with a multiple wick or two candles held together to make one flame, and some spices with a good scent. The traditional blessings of havdalah are available in most prayer books.

For havdalah, wait until the sky is dark enough to see three medium-sized stars and then do the following:

1. Sit quietly with your eyes closed, aware of your body and your breath. Imagine that you are standing in a magnificent garden, filled with fruit and flowers. It is absolutely peaceful here, the temperature is perfect, and there are no dangerous beasts or poisonous insects. Nobody will harm you here; in fact, nobody will even think negative thoughts about you because this is the Garden of Eden.

2. Imagine you can eat the fruits, drink the juices, and smell the fragrances. Imagine that there is a special light in this garden, more penetrating than sunlight, and this light allows you to see the true nature of everything. Thus, you not only enjoy absolute peace in this place, you also experience total awareness.

3. Now, imagine that there is an hourglass with very little sand left in the top half. Time is running out. When the sand is gone, you will have to leave this garden. Only a few minutes remain.

4. Finally, the sand does run out and you find yourself on the other side of the garden's wall. You can still smell its scent, but you can no longer see it. You need to dress warmly now, and you need to be prepared for dangerous beasts and poisonous insects.

5. On the outside of the garden wall is another hourglass that has just been turned. You know that it will run for six days, and then you will be able to return to spend another day in the magical garden. Experience the longing to be back in the garden as you prepare to survive the next six days.

6. Contemplate this for a while, and when you are ready, open your eyes.

As we let go of the Sabbath day, we already begin yearning for the next. Indeed, it is said that the entire purpose of creation is the Sabbath day. The rest is what we need to do to stay alive, but the goal is to be fully present on the Sabbath. It is hoped that our experiences up to this point validate that teaching. Taking time to nourish the soul is usually a wonderful, fulfilling, delicious experience.

The ritual of havdalah is to acknowledge on some level the experience of safety and comfort during the Sabbath day as contrasted with the energy of the busy world. The traditional prayers of the siddur talk about trust and security resting in the embrace of the Divine. The individual family members might at this time acknowledge the trust and love each has for the others.

The havdalah candle with multiple wicks should be lit, or two candles are lit and held together to make one flame. Then someone lifts a glass of wine or grape juice, and offers the traditional blessing: *Baruch attah Adonoi, Elohaynu melach ha-olam, boray pri hagofen.* (Blessed are you, Lord, our God, king of the universe, who created the fruit of the vine.)(As with all the blessings suggested in this book, you can improvise with thoughts of your own, or check a standard Jewish prayer book for other ideas.) One might offer a few thoughts at this time related to anything the wine symbolizes. Some speak of the mysteries of how wine is transformed from grapes, or of the state of mind wine induces, or of its sweetness, and so forth.

The cup is then set back down, without drinking from it, and a container of spices is raised, offering the following traditional blessing: *Baruch attah Adonoi, Elohaynu melach ha-olam, boray minay b'samim.* (Blessed are you, Lord, our God, king of the universe, who creates types of fragrance.) Pass the spices around for everyone to smell. Feel free to improvise to make this moment meaningful for you. Some speak of the spice of life, the indescribable nature of spice, the smell of messianic consciousness, the odor of the Garden of Eden, etc.

Finally, the candles are held up and everyone gazes at their fingertips in the candlelight, while a blessing is offered, traditionally: *Baruch attah Adonoi, Elohaynu melach ha-olam, boray morey ha-aish.* (Blessed are you, Lord, our God, king of the universe, who creates radiant fire.) Some speak here about the extra soul that comes in at the beginning of the Sabbath and departs at havdalah, all of which occurs through the fingertips, or about how the fingers and hands represent action in the world and that we can do good or harm with our hands depending upon our level of consciousness, and so on.

After this, a final blessing is recited: *Baruch attah Adonoi, Elohaynu melach ha-olam, ha-mavdil bain kodesh lekhol, bain ohr le-hoshekh, bain yisrael le-amim, bain yom hash-vi-ii le-sheshit ye-may, ha-mah-aseh. Baruch attah Adonoi, ha-mavdil bain kodesh lekhol.* (Blessed are you, Lord, our God, king of the universe, who separates what is holy from what is secular, between light and darkness, between Israel—that which yearns to go straight to God—and that which doesn't, between the Sabbath and the six days of work. Blessed are you, Lord, who separates what is holy from what is secular.)

Again, use your own interpretation, or even your own blessings. When finished, the leader should drink a mouthful of the wine/grape juice and then extinguish the lights of the candles with the wine, either by pouring it over the lights or by dipping the wicks into it.

At this point the family can join together in a group hug and sing some traditional melodies that are easily learned from friends who do this. This havdalah ceremony closes the Sabbath day.

Kabbalistic Meditations

*Behold, a storm wind [brought] a huge cloud with bright
fire surrounding it, and within it a fire glowed the color of
amber. Also within appeared four living creatures; each like
a man with four faces and four wings...their feet were
straight and hoofed like a calf...under the wings they had
hands...and of their four faces one was the face of a man,
one was the face of a lion, one was the face of an ox, and
one was the face of an eagle. They looked like burning coals
and appeared like torches flashing a bright fire...and they
ran and returned like streaks of lightning.*

Ezekiel 1:4–14

The word Kabbalah means "to receive." On the
esoteric level, it means to receive a transmission
directly from a highly developed teacher, or to
receive an insight from a mysterious force that transcends
reality as we know it. In either case, the transmission can only
be understood if the one receiving is well prepared. In the
kabbalistic metaphor, the receiver is viewed as a vessel, while
the transmission itself is viewed as light.

Most vessels are incomplete, one way or another. They
are "broken" in ways that do not permit much light to be
retained. Like a bowl with a crack from top to bottom that
leaks fluid out as fast as it is poured in, we are also leaky
vessels, losing the light of awareness before we even know

that we have it. It is a given in Jewish mysticism that the light is never diminished; rather the problem is with the vessel's capability to hold the light. Thus, whereas many spiritual traditions are focused on bringing the light of wisdom into the manifest world, Kabbalah is focused on fixing vessels so that the light that is *already here* will be more fully experienced.

Ancient Jewish kabbalists were often named "*merkavah* mystics." The word merkavah means chariot, in this context a symbolic vehicle that gives one access to other realms of reality. Training in the use of this vehicle was referred to as "descent into the chariot." One might think that the correct word should be "*ascent* into the chariot," but this is the point. Whereas ascent signifies reaching beyond ourselves, descent signifies going deep within ourselves, repairing our vessel physically, emotionally, and intellectually, and in this way preparing for journeys to other realms.*

There are many special kabbalistic meditative techniques designed to prepare us for the journey in the chariot and to move us along on the journey itself. One of these techniques is called *yihudim,* "unifications," which takes a number of forms. In one, vowels are chanted aloud, each of which represents a particular part *(sefirah)* of the Tree of Life. At times, these vowels are connected with various names of God, in combinations of sounds and physical movements. One of early practitioners of this method, Abraham Abulafia (thirteenth century), attained extraordinary levels of altered consciousness and ultimately became known as the father of Ecstatic Kabbalah.

Abulafia also used a kabbalistic method he referred to as "gazing," in which he would focus on Hebrew letters, words, or phrases for a long time, and then he would make permutations of the letters or words into new combinations. This led him to discover hidden teachings that opened new worlds. Hebrew lends itself to this method more than other

*See my audiotape series *The Holy Chariot* (Sounds True Audio) for twelve meditative practices that lead to a state of higher consciousness.

languages because of the way it is constructed, primarily built upon three-letter roots. Kabbalists from the beginning have sought out hidden meanings of words in the Torah by switching letters around, by substituting letters of similar shape or sound, or by assigning numeric values to letters and then finding words or phrases with equivalent values *(gematria)*. All of these meditative methodologies lend themselves to deep contemplative exploration.

Some methods of yihudim refer to the mystical results of doing good deeds *(mitzvot)* with the correct state of mind (kavannah). In some prayer books, before doing certain actions, one invites a meditative awareness by saying, "For the sake of the unification *(yihud)* of the [transcendent nature] of the Holy One with the [immanent nature] of the divine presence...to unify *(l'yahed)* the *yod, hey* [the first two letters of the name of God] with the *vav, hey* [the last two letters of this four-letter name], in perfect unity *(b'yihudah)*...[I undertake the following act]." This statement is repeated many times during the prayers, continually inviting a meditative state of mind for the purpose of bringing everything back into oneness.

In the end, on the deepest level, a practitioner is constantly making yihudim no matter what he or she is doing, saying or thinking, for there is a constant awareness of raising holy sparks and merging with the Divine (devekut). Thus, the meditative practices are simply continual reminders to bring one to the ultimate level of consciousness in which there is no real separation.

One of the most important kabbalistic techniques involves using imaginative visualizations. It is a form of active imagination. This technique is derived from the holistic nature of Kabbalah—everything is connected to everything else, in all directions. Although there are descriptions of different dimensions of reality in Kabbalah, these are more related to consciousness than to physicality. In Kabbalah, to go from one dimension of reality to another is not a linear voyage. Rather, it simply requires a shift in consciousness. In the blink of an eye, the kabbalist moves between heaven and hell and what we call this reality. There is no linear time. Past and future are included in this moment. The tool we use to transport ourselves through various levels of reality is called the imagination.

It goes much further than this, however. As noted earlier, kabbalistic perspective suggests that the entire creation is interconnected in such a way that everything that occurs in any part of the creation affects the total picture. There are no isolated acts. Thus, each of us is a reflection of the total universe and everything we do reverberates throughout the universe. When we consider the implications of this for the individual, we realize that things affecting us are happening simultaneously on many layers of reality.

For example, it is obvious that the things that people do around us affect our lives. The closer our relationship with others, the more directly we are affected by their actions. And, of course, vice versa. Now, whereas Kabbalah is concerned with relations between humans and other humans, it is much more focused on the relationships between humans and the Source of Creation, the Divine— the realms of souls, angels, and otherworldly beings. So the question arises: How do our relationships with other realms of reality affect our daily lives? This is where the imagination comes into play, for from the kabbalistic perspective, we are able to communicate with other realms through the vehicles of dreams and imagination.

One of the most basic principles of Kabbalah is phrased: *As above, so below; as below, so above.* We are a reflection of what is happening in the otherworldly realms; and the otherworldly realms are a reflection of what we do here. Therefore, and this is most important, our imagination is not only a tool of reception to know what is happening elsewhere, it is also a tool of transmission, affecting the universe. The power of the kabbalistic meditations that we will be doing, therefore, is two-fold: It reveals the power to us dimensions of ourselves that normally remain locked in the subconscious realms, and it offers us a possibility to heal ourselves on higher dimensions.

Kabbalistic visualizations are more active than many other forms of meditation, for there are no limits to the imagination. It breaks down all barriers of reality. Indeed, most of the barriers we experience are self-imposed. Therefore, you are invited to cut loose the boundaries of your own mind and to enter your imagination with great freedom and inquisitiveness. Every meditation is an exploration of a vast, unknown, new territory.

The guided meditations offered in this book can be used over and over again, each time offering a new experience and a new insight. Some of the meditations can be done on a regular basis and some can be integrated into our lives in a way that completely alters our daily awareness.

One important note: Although these practices with active imagination are often called visualizations, there is no need to actually see anything in your mind's eye. Some people feel that they cannot visualize because they expect to see something on an inner video tube. This is a mistaken understanding. For example, if one suggests that you are on a tropical beach, in an instant most people can recall an experience of being on a beach, but this does not necessarily require a visual image. Rather, it is kind of a thought form. We remember various experiences on different levels: the experience of warmth; the tactile memory of sand; the aural memory of waves; the impressions of breezes, clouds, sky, boats, palm trees—all of this simply as thoughts without particular inner visual reproductions. For some people, the images are indeed visual; for many, however, a combination of the other senses, including thought itself, gives one a clear sense of a tropical beach.

This is the way visualization works. We merely need to think about an image that is suggested and we benefit from this imagination. This is the way you can work with the following meditations.

Jewish meditators have had their own inner virtual reality technique for thousands of years. Nothing can match it. And you are fully equipped to join in this experience. There is nothing to plug into, nothing to add, no helmet to wear, no joystick to hold. The key to this practice is simply to bring your concentration to the process and to let go of your own sense of limitation. It is helpful to be in a quiet, protected place when you do these meditations, so that you can feel secure enough to completely enter them.

It is useful in these practices if you can let go of the inner critic, the editor that lives within all of us. Give yourself full latitude to explore the infinite reaches of the inner world. The kabbalists teach that this is not just your inner world; it is connected with all worlds everywhere. On a meditative level this idea has interesting consequences. The power of imagination is such that anything imagined actually exists not only in our imagination, but in other realms of reality. If we can imagine heaven, then this is real in a very deep way. By allowing ourselves to dwell in these others realms, we gain mystical access. Doubt and cynicism close these realms and keep us bound by our own limitations. A willingness to explore actually opens possibilities, builds faith, and mysteriously rewards the explorer.

Kabbalists love to enter these mystical realms. They are angelic and demonic realms, they are realms where souls dwell, where the divine presence can be directly experienced. They are realms where we can commune with those who are no longer in this world. This is an occult realm that becomes problematic when someone enters it with a desire to control or manipulate the world or anyone in it, including oneself. For this reason, Kabbalah has not only been kept secret for a long time, it has also been feared for its potential occult powers.

When something gets turned into a kind of black magic, it can become dangerous for the practitioner. Abulafia indicated that the use of these techniques with intention to do magical manipulations was not only destined to fail, it was also self-defeating. The purpose of all meditative techniques, including these, is to let go of oneself, to yield and surrender until simply disappearing into the oneness of the source. Thus, the use of magic is frowned upon in Kabbalah. The goal, rather, is to attain "nothingness of thought," as taught by the thirteenth-century kabbalist Azriel of Gerona.

In that spirit, the following kabbalistic meditations are offered to the reader. Many of these are easy to accomplish when read from a book, but they need to be memorized so that you can do them with your eyes closed. It is often helpful to record the meditation on an audio cassette. If working with audio tapes (either pre-recorded* or ones you record for yourself), feel free to turn the tape on and off to spend more time on certain levels.

Some people do these visualizations when going to bed, for they definitely affect our dreams. It is not a good idea, however, to try these when driving or otherwise engaged in activities that require alert interaction.

Many people keep a meditation journal when doing these exercises. It is highly recommended to do so, as you will find that you will make significant progress as the imagination develops and is freed from all constraints. If you have not yet done some of the journaling suggested in the chapter titled "Psycho-Spiritual Journaling" earlier in this book, please do so now before proceeding with the visualizations. This is important training for the work you're about to do. Moreover, when you move ahead with the visualizations, you will surely want to keep a record because, as with dreams, we quickly lose the images and power they contain if we do not spend time reviewing and reflecting upon them at various intervals.

*Most of the meditations in this section of the book are recorded on a two-tape audio series called *Kabbalah Meditation*, produced by Sounds True Audio. A five-tape audio set produced by Sounds True Audio, *The Mystical Kabbalah*, contains the same meditations plus a great deal of information on the basics of Kabbalah.

YIHUDIM CHANTING MEDITATION

(30–60 minutes)

> When Rabbi Eliezer was dying, his students
> visited him. They said to him, "Rabbi, teach us
> the way of life that we will merit eternal life in
> the world to come." He said to them, "Be
> mindful to honor your companions; when you
> pray know before whom you stand; restrain your
> children from idle thought and place them
> between the knees of learned people. For this
> you will merit eternal life."
>
> Babylonian Talmud: *Berachot* 281b

Genesis describes the creation in terms of sound vibration. "And God *said*, let there be light." "And God *said*, let there be a firmament in the midst of the waters." Indeed, we find that the entire creation springs forth from sound.

The Kabbalah is built upon the idea that God's "speech" initially emanates in ten primordial forms, called *sefirot*. The well-known kabbalistic Tree of Life depicts these ten essences and their relationship with one another. The Kabbalah also states that each vowel sound is connected with one of these sefirot. This means that all the power of creation rests in the sounds and vibrations of the vowels.

The consonants in Kabbalah are viewed as garments that hold the creative force of the vowels. In addition, consonants are grouped according to where they are sounded in the mouth. For example, the consonants *b, f, v, m,* and *p* are labials, sounded by the lips. The consonants *c, s,* and *z* are dentals, sounded with the teeth. *D, j, t, l,* and *n* are linguals, sounded by the tongue. *G, y,* and *k* are palatals, sounded by pushing air across the palate. *H* and *r* are gutturals, formed in the throat.

All the vowels are sounded deep in the body. The mouth may form shapes, but the sounding could actually be accomplished without moving the mouth or tongue at all—which is not true of most of the consonants. Try to make the *b* sound without moving your lips, or the *d* sound without moving your tongue. It cannot be done. But you can sound a soft or hard *a, e, i, o,* or *u* hardly moving the mouth at all. The vowels are the most interior sounds of all; they can almost be sounded without the mouth.

In the Kabbalah, every combination of consonants and vowels sends vibrations that have deep esoteric content. All speech and all literature could be analyzed from this perspective. Obviously, this would be a huge study because every word in every language has corresponding vibrations in various combinations of sefirot.

Another concept in the Kabbalah is an important part of this exercise; it is called the Four Worlds. It is said that there are at least four layers of reality, Four Worlds of existence: the world of action *(assiyah)*, the world of formation *(yetzira)*, the world of creation *(beriah)*, and the world of emanation *(atzilut)*. These Four Worlds expand in many metaphors to explain various aspects of creation, and they are a fundamental kabbalistic tool. Each of these worlds has its own soul level: *nefesh, ruah, neshama,* and *chayah.* Let us look more closely at them so that we can gain greater appreciation of the spiritual exercises associated with them.

Assiyah: Nefesh

The world that we are most familiar with is called assiyah, the world of action. This is the manifest universe as we know it. It has substance, dimension, time, and space. It has physical laws. In this world we do things. As we look around us, everything we see is the world of assiyah.

The soul force that permeates this world is called the nefesh. This is a soul that animates, that gives life, movement, and substance to every particle of matter in the universe.

Yetzira: Ruah

The world of formation, called yetzira, is the next level. There is still a sense of time in this world, but spatial perspective is much less apparent. This is the realm of speech and emotions. It is also the realm in which otherworldly creatures exist: angels and demons, fairies and elves, the invisible side of nature. Most of this world is accessible to our senses; we hear speech and we feel our emotions. We also are able to sense the presence of otherworldly creatures, and they can communicate with us in ways that transcend our normal sensory apparatus.

The soul force of this world is called ruah, often translated as "spirit." We can train ourselves through spiritual practice to become highly attuned to the ruah level of the soul, and vast new dimensions open to us when we become sensitized in this way.

Beriah: Neshama

The next level is the world of creation, called beriah. This is a timeless realm, without past or future. It is often correlated with the world of mind—not so much the mind that thinks, but the potential of mind in a universal sense. It is bigger than the individual mind; rather, it is the cosmic mind—mind that is unbounded. Our individual intellectual capacities are connected with the cosmic mind. We put artificial limits upon ourselves by not appreciating the true cosmic nature of mind, and thus the individual approach to mind is greatly constricted.

In its most aware state, the mind has a true appreciation of the oneness of the Source of Creation. Beriah is the realm that we explore in our most advanced contemplative states; it is where the Throne of the Divine is to be found. In the most ancient texts of Jewish mysticism and Kabbalah, the Throne of the Divine represents the highest realms of creation.

The soul force on this level is called neshama—the part within each of us that yearns to be at one with its creator, the part that pulls us on the spiritual path. The neshama is not bounded by ego; rather, it is an aspect of a universal soul-force that resides within each of us, through which all conscious awareness is derived.

Atzilut: Chayah

The highest universe is called atzilut. This is the ephemeral world of emanation. It transcends all form, and indeed it is beyond understanding. It is where the initial conception of an idea takes place. It provides the energy that is needed by the creative world, the world of beriah. This is the world of archetypes, the raw energy of principles upon which creation is based.

The soul identified with the world of atzilut is called chayah, the Living Essence—the mysterious force upon which all life depends, the amazing vitality that empowers a seed to sprout. This is the soul level that is at the center of life, that unfolds like a flower constantly opening, whose center is the very center of the universe.

These are the four essential worlds in Kabbalah. In the most fundamental terms, we can relate these worlds to our lives as our physical reality, our emotional reality, our intellectual reality, and our spiritual reality.

The Four Worlds have many ramifications in Kabbalah, and much of this is based upon the fact that the holiest name of God, the tetragrammaton, is a four-letter word made up of the letters *yod, hey, vav, hey.* Each of these letters represents a world, and, as noted earlier, a great deal of contemplative Kabbalah is designed to do something that unites the lower worlds with the upper worlds, each of which is represented by two of the four letters of this holy name.

Adam Kadmon: Yehida

I should mention that there is also a mysterious fifth world called *adam kadmon.* It is the primordial force of existence that can see to the ends of the universe. It is the essence of total awareness and the source of all will. Without will there can be no energy, without energy there can be no creation, without creation there can be no form, and without form there can be no physical reality.

The level of soul associated with adam kadmon is called yehida, which means "unified." It is the pure force of will within us. The unfolding of this will is the source of creation. It is the oneness.

Sounding the Vowels

Now, let us begin to integrate the kabbalistic approach related to the vowel sounds with a contemplative approach connected to the Four Worlds. For the purpose of this meditation, we will use only three basic vowel sounds and three basic consonants.

According to the Kabbalah, the primary vowel sound associated with the higher sefirot, which could be connected with the third eye and crown, is the sound AH. This represents the third world, the world of beriah, the world of cosmic mind.

The primary vowel sound associated with the center of the chest, the area of the heart, is OH. This represents the second world, the world of yetzira, the emotions and speech.

The primary vowel sound associated with the area of the lower stomach, the base of the spine, is UU (pronounced like the "oo" of pool). This represents the first world, the world of assiyah, the physical plane.

When we sound all three of these vowels in order, we are balancing the three lower worlds, and this leads to equilibrium in the fourth world, the world of atzilut.

Hear these sounds: AH...OH...UU.

The Kabbalah views vowels as light that must be contained in the garments of consonants. The most commonly used garments for contemplative purposes are the consonants that make up the tetragrammaton—the four-lettered unpronounceable representation of the name of God. People have misinterpreted these letters and have sometimes given a name to them—sounding like Yehuvah. But this is not at all what the letters represent. Quite simply, this name of God is not possible to say.

So the kabbalists used the four letters with various combinations of vowels in such a way as to resonate with different attributes of the divine emanation.

The first letter of the holy four-letter name is *y,* the sound of yeh. The next letter is *h,* or hah. The third is *v,* or veh. And the final letter is again the sound of *h,* or hah.

We will begin with the vowel sound of AH, using it with each of the four consonants of the tetragrammaton. As you pronounce these sounds, try to experience the presence of energy in the area of the third eye. Chant each of the following sounds for approximately 10 seconds, and repeat each three times.

YAH HAH VAH HAH

Now to the next. As you say these sounds, try to experience the presence of energy in the center of the chest. It sometimes helps to place a finger on the center of the chest as you make the sound.

YOH HOH VOH HOH

Finally, as you say these next sounds, try to imagine the presence of energy in the lower abdomen, the base of the spine, and the area of the genitals.

YOU WHO VOU WHO

There are numerous rhythms that one could use when saying this mantra. Many overtones can also be brought into the mantra. But the speed or rhythm of the mantra is not as important as pronouncing it clearly and concentrating on the experience of a visualization while making the sounds.

Now, sit straight in a meditative position and follow the chant, doing seven rounds of three times each, in a fairly fast rhythm—about 1 second per sound. You may wish to use your fingers to keep track of the rounds; some people use a string of beads.

It is very important to make an effort to visualize the areas to which the sounds apply. Simply making sounds without a visualization diminishes the power of this meditation. Again, AH vibrates in the area of the third eye, OH in the area of the chest, and UU in the area of the genitals.

Feel free to continue chanting for up to fifty rounds of three times for each of the four consonants: yod, hey, vav, and hey. You may do even more if you wish, but be sure to set a time limit before you begin. When you finish, sit in silent meditation for 5 to 10 minutes and experience the sense of equanimity that results from this practice. Begin now: at least seven, and up to fifty or more rounds.

TEHORA HE/PURE SOUL MEDITATION
(30–45 minutes)

> My soul longs for you in the night, and the spirit
> within me seeks you...the soul within me is
> pure...
>
> Isaiah 26:9 and Morning Prayers

In the preliminary daily prayers of traditional Jewish practitioners, there is a line that says, "My God, the soul which you placed in me, she is pure," or more simply, "The soul within me is pure." In Hebrew the words are: *Elohi neshama shenetatabi, tehora he.*

The following meditation practice focuses on this phrase and the idea behind it—that no matter what we do in this life, the soul within us remains pure. Moreover, no matter whom we encounter, whatever their outward presentation, whatever their personality or history, within each person is a pure soul. Once we fully understand this, our relationship with ourselves and others can be altered, often dramatically.

This and most of the practices that follow will begin with a brief sitting meditation of five to ten minutes to allow yourself to settle down. It is important to develop a degree of comfort in the standard sitting meditation before attempting these visualizations. If you have not done so, please review the section on sitting meditation earlier in this book, then proceed with this meditation. For each of the following instructions, give yourself at least a few minutes; take as much time as you need.

1. Begin with the basic sitting technique: relaxed, eyes closed, sitting fairly straight without effort, breathing normally, noticing the rising and falling of the chest with the breath. Do this for at least 5 minutes.

2. Reflect upon who you are, physically, emotionally, and intellectually, and notice that there are many places of

imperfection. Sometimes we act foolishly, sometimes we say silly things, sometimes we realize that our thoughts are not very kind—indeed, sometimes our thoughts are quite bizarre.

3. As you observe within, notice that you find some things about yourself that are humorous while other things are somewhat unlikable. Notice your feelings.

4. Now, pretend that there is a magic filter so that you can actually see your soul as you would imagine it. Assume this is like a spiritual X-ray machine. You can still see your shape, you can still hear your voice, but the dominant experience is that you are looking straight into your own soul. Notice that self-judgment and self-criticism are not connected with the soul level.

5. Remove the filter and replace your own image with someone else's image. Preferably, try to imagine someone with whom you have had problems or with whom you recently argued. Remembering and reviewing some incident in the past, look and listen carefully as you experience your feelings toward this person.

6. Once again, place the filter between you and this person and say to yourself, "The soul is pure." Notice any change in your feelings toward this person now that you are observing his or her soul.

7. Allow as many people as you wish to appear before you, and then observe them through the filter that says, "The soul is pure." Please do this for a number of people with whom you may have had difficult relations. Continue with as many images as you wish until the time for the meditation is over.

This meditation is extraordinarily useful for opening the heart. It quickly reveals a deeper truth behind the illusion of life, and it teaches us to look more carefully at people and situations; it helps us transcend, to the extent possible, personality and ego.

After you practice it at home, this is a wonderful meditation to take with you into daily life. For each person you encounter, whether a friend or a total stranger, allow yourself to say silently within, "Tehora he" or "This soul is pure." That is all you need do for this practice. Do it regularly and you will quickly find your heart opening. Whenever we acknowledge other souls, we experience our own; moreover, our hearts cannot help but open when we are in touch with our souls. Try it and see.

BITTUL HA-YESH: MEDITATION ON AYIN (NOTHINGNESS) (30–60 minutes)

> And the Lord, your God, will circumcise your
> heart, and the hearts of your offspring, so that
> you will love the Lord with all your heart and all
> your soul in order that you shall live.
>
> Deuteronomy 30:6

One of the Jewish mystics' primary meditative methods parallels a method used by mystics the world over. It has to do with withdrawing from the world, finding a place of inner quiet, and letting go of one's sense of self-identity. It is said that the heart has a covering of psychic material keeping us separated from the inner chambers, which are connected with the Divine. The sheath over the heart is called the ego identity. This meditation practice is used to circumcise the heart, so to speak, to clear away our personal sense of identity so that we can enter the state of nothingness *(ayin)* from which we are able to freely explore the heart's inner chambers.

The word *bittul* means to nullify, to erase. The word *yesh* means somethingness; it is the opposite of ayin. So bittul ha-yesh means to nullify the sense that "I am something," leaving the feeling of nothingness. Although we have an intrinsic feeling that we are somebody or something, this meditation leads us to the truth that we are in fact *not* what we think we are.

Please decide in advance how much time you will allow for this visualization. You can shorten the time if you need, but try not to extend beyond the self-imposed time limit. The reason for this is that the process we are about to do can be quite seductive and the meditator could easily spend many hours in a meditative trance—which is not the purpose. The purpose is to become familiar with your inner world, to discover methods of moving from world to world with the knowledge that there will always be new inner worlds to explore.

It is useful to have a journal handy for this particular meditation because the experience can become quite detailed. From level to level, gateway to gateway, you may wish to interrupt your meditation to record the experiences. This is a worthwhile process, and you will find that you soon become adept at entering into and coming out of the meditative state at will. Thus, in this meditation, reminders will be included for you to record your experience.

1. Begin by sitting quietly, noticing the rising and falling of the chest on the breath for at least five minutes. Then visualize yourself in the middle of an open field. Looking all around, describe to yourself what you see, experiencing it in as much detail as possible.

2. Now, imagine a ladder near you, with its base fixed on the ground, reaching upward into the sky. It reaches beyond where you can see. You know the ladder is very sturdy and safe; it could be climbed if one wished to do so. Please look closely at the ladder, but do not ascend it just yet. Walk around it and describe to yourself what it looks like and how you are feeling at this time.

3. Now, you have the choice of climbing the ladder or ending the visualization. If you choose to end the visualization, open your eyes and record your feelings. If you choose to climb the ladder, stay in the meditation with your eyes closed and describe to yourself the experience and feeling of the first place to which the ladder leads. Please stay at that place. Do not go on. (You may wish to record what you have experienced up to now, and you may continue when finished.)

4. Spend time on this first level. Imagine that you find a gateway, but it is carefully guarded by something or someone. Look closely at the gateway and at the thing or

being that is guarding it. Describe to yourself the situation, what you see, and how it feels.

5. Now, try to discover what you need to do, say, or think in order for this guard to let you through the gate. (You may imagine a conversation with the guard if you wish to ask questions.) Feel free to do whatever you need to find out how to pass through this gate. Continue probing until you discover the necessary key. Any message that arises in your imagination, even the most simple, has meaning for you. (You may wish to record your experience.)

6. Now, once again, you may choose to turn back (as you can at any time) or you may continue. Try to remember your process of decision making. If you turn back, you will end the meditation now. If you choose to go ahead, you will eventually encounter another kind of gate or barrier along the way. Describe your experience, what you see, and how you feel.

7. You can repeat this process until your time runs out. Each time you reach a new level, imagine a gate or something else that is guarded through which you must pass to go on. Find the key each time to get past the block. And every time you reach a new level, rest there so that you can describe it clearly and in detail. Do not rush ahead too fast from level to level. (Record each experience in as much detail as you can recall.)

8. When the time is near for you to finish, please return the same way you entered. That is, reverse your ascent and go back through the levels or chambers you have encountered, always trying to remember what you saw, what you experienced, and what you had to do to get past the gate. It is important to work your way backward, down through the various levels, at the end of this meditation. This reversal and return is an essential part of the process and should not be omitted. When you have returned to the field, open your eyes.

As soon as possible after this meditation, record every-thing that you can remember. Repeat the entire journey in your mind a few times until you have the sequence of events memorized. Then, in moments of reflection during the next week to ten days, review the complete inner voyage. You will find that the review becomes easy and fast—often the voyage can be remembered in less than a minute—and you will begin to become intimately acquainted with the various guardians along the way.

At the end of one or two weeks, you may wish to reenter this visualization and carry it to new levels, or you may wish to begin an entirely new sequence. When a student becomes proficient in this process, the inner pathways can lead to great heights and profound depths.

You will discover that the farther you go in the process, the more you will have to let go of your self-identity. Many of the higher realms are guarded in such a way that one must become almost invisible to enter them. Ultimately, we will begin to experience qualities of the state of nothingness. Thus, this practice, over time, trains us to let go of our selves, so to speak, and allows us profound insight into the nature of our being.

DIVINE PROTECTION (30–45 minutes)

> Like an apple among trees, so is my beloved.
> I sit within his comforting shadow;
> I taste his sweet, refreshing fruit.
> It brings me to a state of inebriation.
> Sheltering me under his love;
> Sustaining me, comforting me;
> I am helpless under his banner of love.
> His left [arm] is under my head;
> His right embraces me.
>
> Song of Songs 2:3–6

The divine protection practice is designed to empower the inner guide that protects us as we go through life. This is also an important place of safety and healing as we engage in other deep meditative practices.

1. Close your eyes and sit quietly, observing the movement of the chest as you breathe. Do this for at least five minutes.

2. Imagine that you are on a wonderful vacation, lying on a beach on a warm sunny day, listening to the surf.

3. Imagine that you are now floating on your back in the water in perfect safety and comfort. You are being supported by an unsinkable foam cushion that is securely fastened to your body. You have absolutely nothing to fear because you are in a bubble of protection and nothing can harm you, yet you can experience nature and the sea around you in their fullness.

4. Now, allow yourself to realize that the cushion and the protection around you are really a form of divine embrace; you are in the arms of God, perfectly safe, relaxed, floating on a sea of love. Enter this experience fully, taking as much time as you wish, dwelling in the embrace of the Divine.

5. Imagine that this is a source of divine protection and is available to you whenever you call on it. Ask it to give you a name, a word, or a symbol by which you will be able to summon it in the future. Let this name, word, or symbol sink deeply into your memory.

6. Now imagine that you are back on the beach, lying in the sun, relaxed.

7. Two or three times, use the name, word, or symbol to enter into the embrace of the Divine, and then come back to the beach. In this way you will become accustomed to summoning the divine protection.

8. When you are ready, open your eyes. Know that your individual angel of protection is always available at a moment's notice.

This meditation of divine protection is often used as a daily practice until it becomes second nature to call upon the light of healing and safety whenever and wherever you feel the need. It is also useful to have instant access to a source of inner protection as you enter more deeply into your spiritual work. There will be times when you want to call on it. The more you practice with this image, the more powerful it becomes.

As we strengthen this image through practice, we begin to realize that it is a major aspect of our intimate guardian angel. In Jewish mysticism, angels take many forms. Sometimes we see them; sometimes they speak with us. Sometimes we know they are present because we feel a strange little nudge. Most of the time we simply experience a presence on a level of intuition, as a mystical experience.

In kabbalistic meditation, we do not have to wait for the guardian angel to make itself known to us; we can call upon it, we can empower it through our inner work, and the amazing vitality of kabbalistic interaction is that the more we empower our guardian angel, the more it empowers us.

In this way, we are able to develop a symbiotic relationship, giving and taking, generating enormous spiritual potential. If you work daily with this power of protection and healing, you will quickly discover its extraordinary benefit.

KABBALISTIC DREAM-HEALING (30–45 minutes)

> R. Huna b. Ammi said: He who has a dream that
> makes his soul sad should go have it interpreted
> in the presence of three. It is argued, however,
> that an uninterpreted dream [with bad news] is
> like an unread letter—it can cause no harm.
> Thus, it is concluded that the dream should not
> be "interpreted" [with anything negative] as
> much as it should be given a "good turn." That
> is to say, the dreamer should go and say: "I have
> had a good dream." The three should respond,
> "It is good and it will be good. May the All-
> Merciful make it good. May it be decreed in
> heaven seven times that it should be good."
>
> *Berachot 55b*

The Talmud discusses dreams at some length—it investigates what they mean and how to deal with them. For the most part, dreams are viewed as openings into other realities, demonic and angelic planes, as well as vehicles for divine revelation. There are many rituals designed for requesting a dream revelation before going to sleep. This you can do in straightforward language as you lie down at night.

The dream-healing meditation is designed to work with dreams that have already occurred. Often our dreams seem mysterious and are difficult to understand. This meditation gives us a method of uncovering hidden messages or deep personal revelations in those dreams. The meditation is best done soon after awakening, while the dream is fresh; but it is also a technique that can be used anytime one wishes to work with highly charged dream images that linger in the memory.

It will help you significantly to do this meditation after you have become accomplished with the divine protection meditation described in the previous pages. Once you are able to raise that image with relative ease, the dream-healing meditation will go much more smoothly. Then you will want to practice the dream-healing meditation until you are able to do it completely from memory. In this way, the next time you have an important dream, you will be able to use this meditation technique immediately after awakening, while the image is still clear.

1. Begin, as usual, with the basic sitting technique: relaxed, eyes closed, sitting fairly straight without effort, breathing normally, noticing the rising and falling of the chest with each breath. Do this for at least 5 minutes.

2. Select a dream that you wish to work with and let the mind review as much of the dream as you are able to remember. Experience the dream as fully as possible. Try not to simply think about the dream, but to re-experience it just as it was when you first dreamed it. Notice the state of your emotions; notice your breathing.

3. Choose one key part of the dream that draws you to it. It may be a mysterious person, a strange event, an emotionally charged moment, or a blocked experience that you were unable to overcome. Try to remember this part of the dream clearly—immerse yourself in it for a minute—and then relax into your meditative breathing. Let go of the dream image altogether. Meditate quietly for a minute or two.

4. Now, invite in the presence of divine protection. Feel your body filling with its glow. Experience an intense gathering of light in the three primary energy centers: the area of the third eye, the center of the chest, and, finally, the lower abdomen. Feel yourself radiating from these three energy centers.

5. Once you are fully surrounded and immersed in the presence of this light, allow yourself to return to the part of your dream that you chose to work with. Notice that with the empowerment of this inner light, you are able to engage

the dream in a new way. Now you are free to work with the dream any way you choose:

a. Perhaps you would like to ask questions of main characters—who they are, what they mean, what message they have for you. If so, try not to mentally edit the answers; listen carefully to whatever is communicated.

b. Perhaps you would like to allow the dream to flow in a new direction, just to see where it will go. If so, allow it to become whatever arises without trying to limit it to the original dream. Let it take you wherever it leads.

c. Perhaps you would like to introduce new elements into a dream event. If so, let your imagination and creativity run freely and see what happens. Do not stay with the original image; whatever unfolds in this meditation has significance for you.

6. Notice that when you are accompanied by the glow of your divine protection, new meaning arises in everything. You are able to get closer to soul-level communications. Trust what happens, and experience the feeling of true protection and healing.

7. Allow yourself now to return out of your dream awareness to your quiet, meditative mind. Watch your breathing. Try to center, balance, relax. Do this for 2 to 3 minutes.

It is best to use this method only once or twice with a single dream, but you can use it with as many separate dreams as you wish. It is very powerful and will inform you on the deepest levels.

Remember, too, never to take literally the messages that come to you in meditation. There is always a hidden meaning in every communication. Our inner being does not usually communicate with us in ways that we normally understand; rather, it uses poetic images, metaphors, parables, symbols, and feelings that must be contemplated to be understood. This is a crucial understanding all spiritual aspirants must attain.

Dream work like this is transformative. It is a way not only to receive messages of divine revelation, but also to engage in higher-realm communication with messages that one wishes to send. Once again, we are working with the kabbalistic principle: *As above, so below.*

When applied to dreams, this kabbalistic concept means that we do not have to be passive recipients of dreams. We can and should be actively engaged in our dreams, working with our imagination in the depths of the psyche and the soul. By doing so, we can actually transform ourselves with our own will and come into greater harmony with the divine will. There is enormous potential for self-healing using this meditative method of working with dreams.

HISHTAVUT/EQUANIMITY (15–45 minutes)

> Praised is the person who finds wisdom and who
> gets understanding. For these are far better than
> silver or gold. She [wisdom] is more precious
> than rubies. There is nothing you could desire
> that could be compared with her. The length of
> your life is in her right hand; her left hand holds
> wealth and honor. Her paths are pleasant ones,
> and all lead to peace. She is a tree of life to those
> who hold on to her and holding her firmly leads
> to happiness.
>
> Proverbs 3:13–18

An ancient Jewish sage, Rabbi Abner, was said to have told the story of an advanced student seeking wisdom at an academy known for the teachings offered by its elders: the Masters of Concentration. When the student was interviewed for admission to the academy, he was asked a crucial question: "Have you achieved *hishtavut* (equanimity)?" The student responded, "What do you mean, master, by hishtavut?" The elder responded, "When someone praises you, does it make you feel good? And when someone blames you, do you feel bad?"

The student thought a while and then said, "When someone praises me, I do feel good for a few moments, and then I let it go. When someone blames me, I do feel bad, and then I let it go. But in either case, I do not treat one more favorably, or hold a grudge against anyone." The old master looked at him and said, "My son, you are doing quite well, but you have not yet achieved true equanimity. You must leave now, and return only when you are able to receive praise or blame without any reaction whatsoever."

This story is well over a thousand years old; its source is unknown. It shows that Jewish mysticism has long held that attaining a high level of equanimity is necessary to achieve higher levels of spiritual consciousness. In many ways, equanimity can only result when the ego has been dissolved. The following meditation helps move one in this direction.

1. Sit quietly with your eyes closed and experience the movement of the chest rising and falling as you center your focus of concentration. Do this for at least 5 minutes.

2. Allow yourself to reflect on up to three major events that arise in your mind that happened to you within the previous two weeks. You may notice that when you are re-experiencing events like this, the rhythm of your breath will change.

3. Pick only one event that you would like to work with during this visualization and reflect on it. Remember it from beginning to end and review it over and over again, reliving the emotion of the event.

4. Imagine that you can bring a new level of wisdom to this event. The wisdom that you can bring is to reflect on all of the variables that led up to this event. Reflect on the nature and background of the people involved in this event and consider the implications of what took place. Allow yourself at least 5 minutes to reconsider the event from these different perspectives.

5. Now, let yourself imagine that anyone else who participated in this event had the same wisdom and understanding of appreciating the immense number of variables that had to coincide and come together to allow this event to take place. They also have the same foresight to appreciate all of the implications that arose as a result of this event having happened. So, now you relive this event under the assumption that you and everyone are participating from this perspective of omniscience. Do this for at least 5 minutes, preferably longer.

6. Say quietly to yourself, "Just as I wish to experience great wisdom, may all the participants in this event experience great wisdom." Notice how this influences your memory of the event.

7. Beginning again, imagine how this event might have unfolded if you had participated in it while filled with the purest sense of lovingkindness; how would things have happened from this perspective? In addition, allow yourself to imagine that all of the participants in the event were filled with lovingkindness; imagine what would have happened. Give this at least 5 minutes.

8. Notice that from the perspective of wisdom, understanding, and lovingkindness, there is a new balance and harmony brought into your memory of the event. Relive the event over and over again through this perspective of balance and harmony. Let your breath become centered, breathing in balance and wholeness, breathing out harmony and peace.

Now come back to the experience of the chest rising and falling on the breath, letting go of the image. Take a couple of deep breaths and open your eyes.

This is a practice that seems to help develop the quality of hishtavut. We learn to see from this that things are more than they seem to be, and that many, many variables must come into play for any event to take place. Appreciating the complexity of each moment is a precondition for higher states of awareness. We find this as well in other traditions.

The practice of hishtavut changes our perspective of events and always brings in the perspective of the soul level, the timeless perspective—what the event really means in terms of the universe. As a kabbalistic practice, it gives us a perception of reality that we don't normally have when we are emotionally entangled in an experience. It leads us to a place of equanimity that brings balance and harmony to our lives.

PROTECTION OF THE ARCHANGELS

(15–30 minutes)

**When a person is about to be born, the angel
Gabriel wrestles with the dust of which the
person is made and introduces into the person
seventy languages. However, the person forgets
[all this wisdom] when entering the world....
Four angels descend into this world with the
person if he or she has a good heritage: Michael,
in the merit of Abraham; Gabriel, in the merit of
Isaac; Uriel, in the merit of Jacob; and Raphael,
in the merit of Adam. The [Shekhina], the good
impulse, is above [this person at all times].**

Zohar Shemot 41b

In Jewish mysticism, each of the archangels represents a divine quality, as if each was a major
emanation of God. When we think of the Divine in terms of
attributes, each attribute is represented by an archangel. This
is a wonderful visualization that is recommended for anyone
seeking protection and security. It is also one of the first
things that is taught to children as a bedtime meditation.

As this meditation is often done when going to sleep, it is
purposely developed here without an endpoint so that the
meditator has the opportunity to continue in the meditation
for as long as he or she wishes. It is a meditation that we can
practice lying down and can fall asleep without feeling
embarrassed. Begin by finding a quiet place to sit or to
lie down.

1. Start the meditation by centering on the breath, but if
you are lying down do not take too long for this as you may
fall asleep before getting to the meditation. Do this for
about 2 minutes.

2. Invoke a sense of the Divine, whatever that means to you. Call to it, "Dear Source of Life, " or, "Dear God of my ancestors, please hear my call."

3. Silently say to yourself, "May the archangel Michael protect my right side, the side of lovingkindness, my expansiveness, my desire to give." As you say this, imagine a presence on your right side, particularly the right side of the head, like a change in air pressure or a tingling on the skin. Anything to sense the experience of a presence on your right side. The archangel Michael represents divine generosity.

4. Silently call out again. "May the archangel Gabriel be on my left side, the side of restraint, where I have my protection, and where the strength of my creative force resides." Feel the presence on your left side, again particularly on the left side of your head. Imagine something is there, embracing you on the left, just as on the right. The archangel Gabriel represents the power and strength of God.

5. Slowly and silently invoke, "May the archangel Uriel be in front of me, the balance point of my wisdom and my understanding; where knowledge resides." Imagine the presence of a light in front of you. Uriel represents the divine light.

6. Silently say to yourself, "May the archangel Rafael stand behind me at my foundation." Imagine the presence of a strongly supportive and healing force behind you, especially near the tailbone. The archangel Rafael represents the divine healing power.

7. Now you are completely embraced: on your right by Michael, the power of lovingkindness; on your left by Gabriel, the power of strength; in front of you, Uriel, the divine light; behind you, Rafael, the divine healing. Let yourself sink into the experience of this divine embrace.

8. Finally, silently invoke, "And may the presence of God rest above my head and above my body. The Shekhina, the divine feminine presence of God, surrounding me, enveloping me, embracing me." Completely immerse yourself in this experience for as long as you wish.

9. Feel the presence on your right, on your left, and behind or beneath you. Imagine a bright light in front of you. Notice an all-encompassing presence over you, surrounding you, holding it all together. Feel the safety of this embrace. The comfort. The security. The love. The peacefulness. Melting into it. Surrendering. Letting go totally. Floating in the arms of God....

TESHUVAH: RETURN OF THE SOUL

(45–60 minutes)

> A person who merits punishment will be saved only if he or she has great advocates, otherwise not. What are the advocates? Teshuvah (repentance) and good deeds. [These are so powerful], even if nine hundred and ninety-nine [misdeeds] argue for punishment and only one argues in the person's favor, the person is saved.
>
> *Shabbat* 32a

This is a meditation to make what is called a *chesbon ha-nefesh* (a reckoning of the vital soul); it is a meditation for self-evaluation. In Judaism, this kind of self-evaluation is done at regular intervals. It is especially important to do at the time of the year of the High Holy Days of Rosh Hashana and Yom Kippur. The purpose of doing a cheshbon ha-nefesh is to gain insight into how we are doing and to consider new directions for raising ourselves to ever higher levels of consciousness.

1. Find a comfortable, quite place to sit and allow your attention to come to the experience of the body. Let your attention come to the rising and falling of the chest as you breathe in and breathe out. Do this for 5 minutes.

2. Let yourself imagine that you are standing in a field. Off to one side is a ladder that reaches into the heavens. Imagine that it is a ladder that is safe for you to climb. When you are ready, begin to ascend the ladder up to a place out of sight…climbing…climbing…until you arrive at a plateau.

3. This plateau is a large amphitheater that has two tables in the middle. Surrounding it are heavenly beings of all types and forms. You are standing near one of the tables in the center of the amphitheater.

4. There are two other beings with you here. One is an accuser, like a prosecuting attorney. The other is a defender. It is now that you realize that you are on a kind of trial. It is not a final trial, but a mock trial. It is a rehearsal. And you are going to have an opportunity here to see what the accuser has to say about you, and what the defender has to say.

5. Feel the experience of being here, on trial for your life, in this large amphitheater. Both the accuser and defender know every single thing about you that you know about yourself. They know everything you've ever done, every action, every word, every thought.

6. The accuser is going to make three accusations about you. Listen carefully to what the accuser says about the way you have lived your life up until now. Be sure to limit it to three accusations even though there may be many more. (approx. 2–3 minutes)

7. Notice how it feels when you hear what is being said about you. Notice what the accuser looks like.

8. Now it is time for your defender to respond to the three accusations. The defender is able to reach back into the past for things you may have done that aid in arguing your defense. Notice what the defender looks like and listen to what it has to say. (approx. 2–3 minutes)

9. Notice how you are feeling as the defender speaks for you.

10. Now it is time once again for the accuser to make one final statement about you, one strong accusation. Listen carefully to what it says. (approx. 2 minutes)

11. Let your defender make one final statement in your defense. Hear what it says. (approx. 2 minutes)

12. Finally, you now have an opportunity to speak in your own defense. You can make whatever promises seem important to you regarding the rest of your life. Listen to

yourself. What are you willing to do to live a life of higher consciousness? Listen to what you say now, in this amphitheater, to all the heavenly beings that are surrounding you, as you speak in your own defense. (approx. 3 minutes)

13. Now, remembering what you said and turning back to the ladder that brought you here, allow yourself to descend back into the field. When you have arrived, remember the experience of having been here before. Look around. When you are ready, take a deep breath or two and open your eyes.

This is a very useful meditation for checking in to discover your inner feelings of guilt and pride, to determine what you are willing to do to go to higher levels of consciousness. It is very useful to keep a record of your experiences when you do this meditation. You may want to take a few moments to write down what the accuser said, what the defender said, and, of course, what you said to the heavenly tribunal.

This meditation should be done at least once, but no more than a few times a year, When doing it, give it plenty of time. After completing, it is useful to try to remember it a few times each day for the week or two immediately following the experience. In this way, one connects quickly with one's own feelings and establishes firmly one's commitment to transform oneself. This is a powerful method, even when only done a few times a year.

RAISING HOLY SPARKS (30–45 minutes)

> The infinite primordial light spread radiance on
> everything and as it spread to all sides, the light
> shot out sparks. God stored these away for the
> righteous. Why? So that the righteous could
> bring forth fruit from these sparks. Thus it indeed
> happened that they brought forth fruit in the
> world. For Abraham and Sarah "made souls"
> (Genesis 12:5). Just as they made souls from the
> Holy Side [the "good" side of creation], so too
> did they make souls from the Other Side [the
> "evil" side of creation]. For if this influence of
> the Other Side were not in this world, there
> would be nothing to overcome [and therefore no
> real free choice to do good].
>
> *Zohar Shemot* 147b

The Baal Shem Tov teaches that all things have within them holy sparks. We have to learn to see through the hard shells of creation to discover holy sparks hidden inside so that we can raise them up to their origin and ultimately attain messianic consciousness. The following is a guided meditation to give us ideas for identifying these sparks and what we have to do to raise them up.

1. Sit quietly with your eyes closed, attending the breath, noticing the body. Do this for 5 minutes.

2. Allow yourself to think of someone that you know quite well, and think about no more than three of his or her personality traits that you really like—the three most likeable, positive things that your know about this person.

3. Now allow yourself to think of one or more attributes that you really find unpleasant about this person, something that makes you uncomfortable that you wish could be changed. If there are more than one, pick the one that you dislike the most and focus on it. On the other hand, if you are

unable to identify anything unpleasant, choose a different person for this exercise, and then repeat steps 2 and 3.

4. Look deep within yourself to see if you can determine what it is about the unpleasant trait or characteristic that really bothers you. What do you identify with it? What kind of fear does it raise in you? It might help to imagine what it would be like if you, yourself, had this trait. How would you relate to it and how would others relate to you? Use your imagination. Imagine yourself with this trait and see how it feels.

5. Imagine yourself with this trait that is unlikable and see if you can discover within it something useful, something nourishing, something that it accomplishes. Imagine that it is a gift, this trait, a gift from the Divine. When you are able to open the gift and see deep within, you will discover a profound truth. So what is the truth hidden deep within this characteristic that you find so uncomfortable?

6. Now that you have discovered that this attribute contains something of truth from the Divine, once again allow yourself to reflect upon the person who has this trait. Let yourself now experience this person with this characteristic or attribute, noticing how you feel about him or her.

7. You will probably notice that your feelings have changed somewhat. If so, this is called "raising the sparks." Stay with these feelings for a little while and notice how those inner edges of criticism and judgment soften when your understanding deepens about the sparks hidden within everything.

Do this exercise again for others with different personality traits. Notice that there is always some kind of redeeming sparks to be found in almost everything. After completing these meditations, reflect on them as often as you remember to do so. Especially think about this when you encounter people in daily life who have unpleasant characteristics and see if you can modify your reactions on the spot. This is what it takes to identify holy sparks and raise them up. Do this meditation exercise whenever you feel yourself becoming alienated and critical. It is another technique for softening the heart.

FOUR WORLDS (30–45 minutes)

> There are four sacred and mighty beings called
> Hayyoth [life forces] who hold up the
> firmament.... They sing "Holy, holy, holy, is
> Adonoy Tzevaot (the Lord of Hosts), the whole
> world is full of Its glory" (Isaiah 6:3). They turn
> to the south and say "holy," they turn to the
> north and say "holy," they turn to the east and
> say "holy," they turn to the west and say
> "blessed."
>
> *Zohar Bereshit* 71b

As previously discussed, Kabbalah offers an image of creation in the form of Four Worlds: atzilut, beriah, yetzira, and assiyah. Atzilut is the world of spirituality, beriah is the world of the intellect, yetzira is the world of emotions and speech, and assiyah is the world of physicality. There are many metaphors dealing with these Four Worlds and basic kabbalistic techniques to reflect upon various events and people from the perspective of the Four Worlds. The following Four Worlds meditation will give you an example of how this works.

1. Once again, sit quietly, observing the breath rising and falling in the chest or the stomach. Don't be concerned when other thoughts arise as you are sitting quietly. Just allow them to come and go as you continuously bring your consciousness to the physical experience of the rising and falling of the chest or stomach. Do this for 5 minutes.

2. Visualize yourself, your physical being, your physical strengths and weaknesses. How are you built? Are you tall? Are you short? Are you thin? Are you chubby? Are you strong? Notice when doing this the tone of the inner voice. Are you objectively evaluating yourself, or is there a subjective, judgmental, self-critical tone? As the purpose of this particular meditation is simply to be objective, please be

careful not to enter into a judgmental state of mind. Simply be objective in noticing your physical strengths and weaknesses. What is this body of yours best designed to do; what are some things it cannot do so well?

3. Next, analyze yourself on the emotional level. Emotionally, what are you well suited for, and what would be difficult assignments for you? Again, view yourself objectively, as if you were someone else applying for a position and you had to report on this person's emotional makeup. How do you do with stress, frustration, anxiety, love, friendship, authority, and so forth?

4. Now move up to the level of the intellect. What is your mind good for, and in what are you less intellectually competent—from your own objective perspective? Report to yourself on your intellectual strengths and weaknesses. Again, be careful not to fall into the trap of being self-critical or self-judgmental. The purpose of this exercise is not to feel bad or uncomfortable about who we are, but simply to evaluate our inherent skills and abilities. In which situations does your intellect serve you well, and where is it lacking— from your perspective?

5. Now we are going to take a little journey back in time. Pretend and imagine that you are able to enter into the higher soul levels. What was your soul before you were born? This may be difficult to visualize so simply pretend that whatever you experience are souls and not people.

6. Imagine that your soul and others are seated at a large table. All of these souls are in some way related to you: your parents, your brothers, your sisters, your lovers, your friends. You are all seated at this table before any of you were born and you are discussing what it is you need to do that requires joining a body in the world. You all need to do something, fix something, or accomplish something. You may not be able to articulate this completely, but you know that you have made a commitment to join a particular body, to have relationships with these other souls, to accomplish some fixing in yourself and in the world.

7. Now return to your present body and once again reflect on your physical structure, your emotional makeup, and your intellectual capacity. Look at all these things now in terms of the idea that you have inherent attributes that are precisely what your soul needed in order to accomplish exactly what it had to do in this world. Say to yourself, "I have exactly what I need."

8. Now, consider what it would mean if there were no mistakes whatsoever in your choice of physical, emotional, and intellectual makeup. Assume that your soul chose this body you are in. You have been given exactly what you need in terms of your physical, emotional, and intellectual strengths; and you have exactly what you need in terms of your family relations. Everything you have is precisely what you need to make the repair of your soul and of the world; this is something that was determined before you were born. Please contemplate this for a few minutes.

9. When you are ready, allow your imagination to relax. Come back to the experience of observing your chest rising and falling on the breath. Notice if there is any tension in your arms and hands, in your head, neck, and jaw. Relax for a couple of moments, and when you are ready, end this meditation.

The Four Worlds meditation is designed to help us realize that everything in our lives operates harmoniously with the higher realms, that all our characteristics are integrated in the unified wholeness of who we are. We have exactly what we need to perform the task that we are here to do, whatever it may be. This is an empowering meditation, strongly suggesting that our lives are not accidental, our relationships with friends and family are not random. Moreover, we realize that everything we have and every event we experience is a gift, once we gain an understanding of the cosmic perspective.

INNER HARMONY (30–45 minutes)

> For everything there is a season and a time to
> every purpose under heaven: A time to be born,
> and a time to die; a time to plant, and a time to
> harvest...to weep, to laugh, to mourn, to
> dance...to seek, to lose, to keep, to cast
> away...to rend, to sew, to keep silence, to
> speak...but there is nothing better than to rejoice
> and do good in this life.
>
> Ecclesiastes 3:1–12

This meditation is dependent upon the Tree of Life, which is reflected in the human body. There are three power points that represent three of the primary forces on the Tree of Life. These are the same three points that were used in the yihudim meditation earlier (see page 130). One of these power points is between the eyes, one of them is in the center of the chest around the sternum, and one of them is in the lower abdomen about half way between the navel and the genitals, corresponding to the base of the spine. These three power points reflect the balancing of opposites on the Tree of Life. This meditation gives one wisdom in learning to use these points for balancing oneself. In the yihudim meditation, we used chanting of vowels to balance these power centers. In this inner harmony meditation, we similarly balance the power centers, but we do so silently, using tactile imagery.

1. Sit quietly with your eyes closed. Notice the chest rising and falling. Allow thoughts to arise and fall, and gently return the focus to the rising and falling on the chest. Do this for 5 minutes.

2. Let yourself sway gently in all directions until you find a point of balance between forward and back, right and left, a point of equilibrium. This feels like a perfect balance point.

3. Imagine that you can be aware of the right side of your head, your right ear, your right cheek, your right eye, your right temple. You can actually feel and locate the right side of the head. Now let that go and reverse your awareness to the left side of the head. Notice the left ear, left temple, left cheek, and left eye. Allow your awareness to rest precisely in the mid-point between the right side and the left side of the head, and imagine that point located somewhere near the third eye. You may experience it as a point, or a line, or an actual plane, and allow energy to radiate in that area.

4. Now let the energetic feeling extend downward. Find the center-point between the right and left side of the torso. Find a point of perfect balance somewhere in the area of the breastbone, heart, and solar plexus. Let your imagination flow with the tactile sensation of a line of perfect balance from the center of the head down to the center of the torso, connecting the two points from the third eye to the center of the chest.

5. Continue the extension of this line downward to the area around the base of the spine, near the genitals, the lower abdomen, balancing the lower half of the torso, the right side and left side.

6. Feel the energy radiate in the area of the third eye; feel the energy radiate in the center of the chest, near the solar plexus; feel the energy radiate in the lower abdomen; and connect these three radiating power points with a line on the center of balance.

7. Feel the balance of everything on the right and left. Allow the line to extend upward through the crown of the head, upward to the center of everything, and allow it to extend downward through the genitals into the earth, downward to the center of everything. The body is in perfect balance and harmony with this line that loops through the center of everything.

8. Come back to the experience of the breath, allowing the image of the line to dissolve, coming present. Take two or three deep breaths and open your eyes.

On a practical level, one of the things we learn kabbalistically is whatever issue presents itself to us, there is always a balance point for our experience. There is always another side to the story. There is always something deep that we can connect with. And so, we do this practice of meditation on inner harmony, especially in times when we are engaging stressful situations to get greater clarity. This is another form of raising holy sparks. But it is accomplished through tactile bodily experiences rather than intellectually. The important focus of this meditation is the physical experience of radiating energy.

When engaged in this meditation, we can rest at the point where the line is clearly developed, reaching from heaven to earth, passing through the center of our being, and we can invite in at that point any difficult situation in which we are absorbed at that moment. When we do so, we gain a new perspective on the relationship that has developed and perhaps a new appreciation for the situation.

The advantage of this method is that we can do it silently and even with our eyes open. Thus, it is an excellent method to experience in public. It calms the mind in tense situations and helps us respond clearly. It is strengthened, however, when we are alone by coordinating it with the chanting of the yihudim meditation.

The focus on the balance points of our body helps develop a new sense of harmony, neither leaning to one side of an issue nor another. Not leaning forward into the future, or backward into the past. It is an experience that transcends the intellect and relies much more on the wisdom of the body. In this sense it cannot be explained, but it is understood on a much deeper plane.

SHADOW OF GOD (30–45 minutes)

> Bezelel [the builder of the Tabernacle] was so
> wise, he knew how to combine the Hebrew
> letters by which heaven and earth were created.
> As a result of his great wisdom, he was set apart
> to build the Tabernacle.... He was set apart
> above as well as below.... For his name was
> Bezelel, that is b'zel El, "in the shadow of God."
> Who does he represent? The Tzaddik (the
> "righteous one") who sits in the shadow of the
> One whose name is "the highest God" (El
> elyon).
>
> *Zohar Shemot* 152a

The Jewish mystics call nature by the name *zel Shaddai*. Zel means shadow, and Shaddai is one of the many names of God.* It is taught in the oral tradition that at the heavenly throne there is a curtain that hangs before the infinite light. Woven into this curtain are all of the events of the past, the present, and all of the events of the future, everything that has ever happened and will ever happen. And every soul that exists in the universe is also woven into this curtain. We are going to use this basic mystical teaching of the curtain as the primary image source for this visualization.

1. Begin relaxed, eyes closed, sitting fairly straight, breathing normally, noticing the rising and falling of the chest. Do this for at least 5 minutes.

2. Imagine you are an observer at the heavenly throne. On one side there is a very bright light shining through a curtain that has images woven into it. On the other side of

---

*Note that Bezelel, from the quote above, represents one "face" of God called El elyon, while Shaddai represents a different face of God. Thus the shadow of El elyon will have a different quality than the shadow of Shaddai, even though both are called the "shadow of God." The different "faces" *(partzufim)* of God are discussed at length in my book *God Is a Verb* (Riverhead, 1997).

the curtain there is a large curved wall of glass upon which shadows of the images of the curtain are cast. The shadow you watch looks like a person.

3. Notice that when the light and the curtain are still, the shadow is still. Notice that when the light moves, the shadow moves. Notice also that if the light is still but the curtain moves, the shadow still moves on the curved wall.

4. Imagine this is a big amphitheater and the curved wall in the center is actually a sphere of glass. The shadows on this glass can be seen from all directions. When both the light and the curtain move very rapidly around this sphere, the shadows cast on the sphere seem three dimensional. They seem almost to have their own personality and movements. If we did not know they were shadows, they would seem to be real. Once again, if this is difficult to imagine visually, simply pretend that you can think of people living in a glass ball who are really nothing more than moving shadows.

5. Now amplify your imagination and pretend that a shadow you are watching has substance. This substance is called consciousness and it has its very own light source. Thus, the so-called shadow has its own consciousness, and has at its center its own light. If the shadow has its own substance, then the light at its center would cast its shadow back on the curtain. It would be a shadow of a shadow, so to speak, and so it adds a new form to the weave on this mystical curtain.

6. Let yourself sit with the feeling of a light shining within you. Sit with this for a few minutes.

7. Let go of the image. Come back to the experience of the breath. Take one or two deep breaths and open your eyes.

This visualization represents the basic nature of reality according to Kabbalah. Everything is a shadow that appears in three dimensions. Its apparent substance is given by the light of God that passes through a primordial archetype. This image of a light shining though a curtain of archetypes, creating the universe, represents the Ohr Ein Sof, the infinite light of awareness. The universe is dependent upon this light shining continuously, which means that each moment is a moment of creation. All of creation receives its form from this light.

The aspect of creation that has consciousness in the sense that we know it as humans also has a light, a spark of the Divine within itself, that casts an image back on the curtain, continuously setting new images. Thus, the curtain not only has the images of archetypes placed there for eternity, but it also constantly changes with the addition of images cast upon it by the consciousness that inhabits this universe.

This continuously changing design on the curtain represents the unfolding of creation from moment to moment, constantly in process, dependent as much on our consciousness as on the original light. No one stands alone, and everyone plays an important role. Everything in the universe is connected. Moreover, we always live in full partnership with the Source of All Creation.

This is an empowering idea. At the same time it is terrifying, for we now must shoulder our share of the responsibility for the destiny of the world. It is in our hands as much as it is in God's hands, for the two are inseparable. A shadow cannot be separated from its source. It moves in perfect harmony with its source. In essence, it is its source. This is our relationship with the Divine from the kabbalistic perspective.

TIKKUN: HEALING THE DEAD (30–45 minutes)

> Raba was sitting near the bed of Rav Nachman
> when he [Nachman] was in his last breaths of
> life. Rav Nachman said to Raba, "Please urge
> [the angel of death] not to cause me any pain."
> Raba replied, "Are you not yourself a friend [of
> the angel of death, and therefore could ask him
> yourself]?" Nachman replied, "Who can contend
> at such a time as this?" Raba then requested,
> "[After you are on the other side] please let your
> soul appear before me [when I am dreaming, so
> that I can discover something of your passage]."
> [After the death of Nachman, his soul appeared
> to Raba in a dream.] When it appeared, Raba
> asked: "Did you have any pain [in the
> transition]?" Nachman answered: "It was as easy
> as removing a hair from milk."
>
> Babylonian Talmud: *Mo'ed Katan* 28a

This visualization of healing the dead is unique in that we are able to not only work on our own spiritual development, but we can also influence, in kabbalistic terms, soul forces that have passed over into other realms. This has profound kabbalistic content in the sense that we can work with energy on an entirely different level of existence. This meditation is based on the idea that time is relative and that even though a soul force may have passed into the other realm, we can still influence it from this realm of reality. Indeed, the primary advantage of being alive in this world is having free will. This being so, we can accomplish some things in this reality of existence with our free will that soul forces cannot achieve in realms that lack free will.

Let your imagination flow with this. You will discover it to be a useful and significant meditation that will cause healing on many different levels, and you will find that it will bring a new realization in terms of your relationship with someone who has left this world.

1. Begin by sitting relaxed, eyes closed, breathing normally. Do this for at least 5 minutes.

2. Bring into your imagination someone who is deceased. It can be a close friend or a relative; it can be someone who passed away recently or long ago. The important thing is that it should be someone you personally knew when he or she was alive. Bring this image into your imagination, remembering the person.

3. Notice your emotions. Notice if you are feeling sad. Now allow yourself to rise above your emotions so that you can enter into an objective frame of mind, a place of equanimity. Imagine your soul and the soul of the deceased one are having a conversation, and let the one who is deceased tell you, briefly, what it feels it accomplished when it was alive. Do this for a few minutes.

4. Now, let the other soul tell you what it feels it failed to accomplish. Let it tell you what its shortcomings were when it was alive. Do this for a few minutes.

5. Imagine saying to this soul, "If there were one thing that could be done at this time, one fixing that could be made for something you failed to do when you were alive, what would that one thing be? What would you change about your life, if you could?" Listen carefully to what this soul tells you.

6. Now, using the full range of your imagination, imagine that you are doing the very thing that this soul tells you it needs to do. Do this for the soul. That is, imagine what it would have been like for this person when he or she were alive, had this one thing been done. Once you are able to envision this in your mind, replay it over and over again, with as many variations on a theme as you need in order to make this image complete. In other words, you are recasting your memory of this soul in a way that imagines the person to be who you believe he or she would have wanted to be. Do this for at least 5 minutes.

7. Notice your emotions and your breath. If you are feeling your emotions and you are breathing differently, your imagination is deeply engaged. Now come back to the balanced breath. Let go of all the images. Observe the chest rising and falling. Take two deep breaths and open your eyes.

You can repeat this process a few times with this soul, but it is not recommended to continue for too long or to return to the same soul too often. This tikkun (fixing) is accomplished quickly and one can feel free to move on without dwelling more than the amount of time designated above. Thus, do not repeat this exercise more than a couple of times a month, at the most.

This is a highly recommended meditation, especially for people who have recently lost loved ones. It has a powerful impact on your soul and on the soul of your loved one. We can do things in this world, we can actually continue the process of the tikkun, the fixing, that the departed soul set out to do. The kabbalistic ramifications run quite deep in this meditation. Work with it. Try it out. See what happens.

DEVEKUT: MELTING INTO THE DIVINE

(30–45 minutes)

> The creator holds securely to the upper world
> and also to the lower world. He does not court
> the female [the creator does not have to entice
> creation], since one never parts from the other
> and both are eternally in a state of
> interconnectedness. The seed could not flow
> except when it can be received [giving cannot
> operate independently but always flows when
> continuously received], and so it is that the
> mutual desires [of both giver and receiver] are
> blended into one inseparable ecstasy [every
> moment of creation].
>
> *Zohar Bereshith* 162b

One of the central practices in Jewish mysticism is the idea of letting go of the sense of self so that we are able to become at one with the Source of Creation—at one with the Divine. This, as noted before, is called devekut. It is probably one of the most discussed meditative practices in the Hasidic movement and in all of Kabbalah. The visualization that follows is one of many ways to enter into the mind state of devekut.

1. Sit quietly where you will not be disturbed for 30–45 minutes, body relaxed, eyes closed, experiencing the breath. Do this for 5 minutes.

2. Imagine you are standing in a field, a meadow. In one direction you can see a dwelling in the distance. Approach the dwelling without going inside. There is nobody living here at this time and it has at least three rooms inside. You may circle it if you wish, but in any case, describe to yourself what it looks like from the outside.

3. Now, enter the dwelling and go into the first room you see. The room is completely empty except for a large

full-length mirror hanging on one wall. Stand before this mirror and look at yourself. See yourself as other people see you. Evaluate yourself physically, emotionally, and intellectually as you see yourself in the mirror. See the strengths and weaknesses of your personality in this mirror. Notice how you feel.

4. Step back and make your way into a second room. This room is darker than the first and also empty. It, too, has a full-length mirror. As the light begins to grow in this room, realize that you are going to be able to see an image of the Divine reflected in this room's mirror. Looking deeply into this mirror you are going to be able to see one of the infinite images of God, however it represents itself to you. Try not to be judgmental of the image. Simply allow it to be whatever arises. Any image (or non-image) is fine. Feel the presence of God in this room.

5. Slowly step back from the mirror, gather yourself, and begin to make your way into the third room, which is quite dark when you first enter. In this room, notice that it, too, is empty and there is a full-length mirror on the wall. As the light begins to brighten you will notice that you are looking at yourself, once again, except that you are now able to see yourself through the eyes of the Divine. You are able to see your physical, emotional, and intellectual makeup through the eyes of God. Let the room fill with light, complete and bright. Let your heart completely open to this image of yourself as seen through the eyes of God, for this is the true nature of your being.

6. When you are ready, let yourself go back out the same way you came into this dwelling. Let yourself go back to the field where you began this journey. Notice now how it feels to be here. Feel in yourself the sense of your true nature, and know that you can live your life as if you are always viewing yourself and everything around you through the eyes of God. Every action that you make, every word that you speak,

every thought in your mind, through the eyes of God. It will transform you. It will transform your relationships with those around you. And it will transform your relationship with the Divine. Thus, regarding devekut it is taught:

> After the Sabbath meal was completed, Rabbi Simeon bar Yohai [one of the most famous Jewish mystics] would arrange his table and meditate on the workings of the chariot *(ma-asey merkevah)* [which reveals the secrets of the creation]. He would say, "This is the king's banquet; *let him join me.*" Thus, the Sabbath is superior to all other feast days for it has a unique kind of holiness.... On the Sabbath all sadness, annoyance, and trouble are forgotten because on this day [we experience] the divine presence [of the Shekhina] and an additional soul *[neshama yetirah]* is given to us.
>
> *Zohar Vayikra* 95a

Shabbat is our time every week of devekut, to let go of our old selves, our cares, our worries, and to "en-joy," to allow our additonal soul to bring a universal joy into our hearts, filling us with gratitute, love, and harmony. May we all experience Shabbat and other days of rest so that we can join together in manifesting messianic consciousness for all beings to appreciate a new peace of mind. May we all be blessed to experience this in our lifetimes.

And let us say: Amen.

Appendix 1

Psalms: Selections for Reflection and Memorization

(Transliterated and Translated)

T he following phrases can be used as mantras, to be repeated while in a state of meditation. A mantra's rhythm is important, as is its pronunciation. If possible, try to work with the Hebrew sounds and develop a rhythmic rendition by adding any melody that comes naturally. The English translation adds the dimension of conceptual understanding, but as with all translations of holy language, the English falls short of the deeper meanings. These deeper messages will come in the context of the meditation as the phrase is repeated over and over.

One important note: The words Lord and It are used here to follow conventional translations. However, the meditator should feel free to substitute her or his own image of the Divine wherever it fits—images such as Mother, Source, Infinite Nothingness, God, Unity, Force, Being, the Unconditioned, the Unborn, the Unknowable, and Reality.

כִּי־עִמְּךָ מְקוֹר חַיִּים בְּאוֹרְךָ נִרְאֶה־אוֹר׃

Ki imkha mekor chayim, b'orkha nireh ohr
For with you is the source of life, in your light we see light.
PSALM 36:10

מַה־יָּקָר חַסְדְּךָ אֱלֹהִים:

Mah yakar chasd'kha, Elohim
How precious is your lovingkindness, Lord.
PSALM 36:8

יְהֹוָה הוֹשִׁיעָה הַמֶּלֶךְ יַעֲנֵנוּ בְיוֹם־קָרְאֵנוּ:

Adonai hoshi'ah, hamelekh ya'aneinu b'yom koreinu
Save [us] Lord, Almighty, answer us on the day we call.
PSALM 20:10

טוֹב־יְהֹוָה לַכֹּל וְרַחֲמָיו עַל־כָּל־מַעֲשָׂיו:

Tov Adonai lakol, v'rachamav al kol ma'asav
The Lord is good to everything, and has mercifulness on all of Its creation.
PSALM 145:9

יְהֹוָה מַתִּיר אֲסוּרִים: יְהֹוָה פֹּקֵחַ עִוְרִים

יְהֹוָה זֹקֵף כְּפוּפִים יְהֹוָה אֹהֵב צַדִּיקִים:

Adonai mattir asurim, Adonai pokay'ach ivrim, Adonai zokeif kefufim,
Adonai ohev tzaddikim
The Lord releases those who are bound, the Lord opens [the eyes of] the blind, the Lord raises those who are bent, the Lord loves the righteous.
PSALM 146:7

עֱנוּ לַיהֹוָה בְּתוֹדָה זַמְּרוּ לֵאלֹהֵינוּ בְכִנּוֹר:

Enu Ladonai b'todah, zamru Leloheinu b'khinor
Sing to the Lord in thanksgiving, sing to our Lord with a harp.
PSALM 147:7

יְהַלְלוּ שְׁמוֹ בְמָחוֹל בְּתֹף וְכִנּוֹר יְזַמְּרוּ־לוֹ׃

Y'hallelu sh'mo v'machol, b'tof v'khinor y'zamru lo
Let them praise Its name with dance, let them sing to It with cymbals
and harp.
    PSALM 149:3

כֹּל הַנְּשָׁמָה תְּהַלֵּל יָהּ הַלְלוּיָהּ׃

Kol haneshamah t'halleil Yah, Halleluyah
Let every breath praise the Lord; praise It!
    PSALM 150:6

לְעֹשֵׂה אוֹרִים גְּדֹלִים כִּי לְעוֹלָם חַסְדּוֹ׃

L'oseh orim g'dolim, ki l'olam chasdo
To the maker of great lights, for Its lovingkindness is eternal.
    PSALM 136:7

אֲדֹנָי שְׂפָתַי תִּפְתָּח וּפִי יַגִּיד תְּהִלָּתֶךָ׃

Adonai s'fatai tiftach u'fi yaggid t'hilatekha
Lord, open my lips and my mouth will praise you.
    PSALM 51:17

נְצֹר לְשׁוֹנְךָ מֵרָע וּשְׂפָתֶיךָ מִדַּבֵּר מִרְמָה׃

N'tzor l'shonkha mei-ra, u-s'fatekha midabber mirmah
Keep your tongue from evil and your lips from speaking deceitfully.
    PSALM 34:14

גַּדְּלוּ לַיהוָה אִתִּי וּנְרוֹמְמָה שְׁמוֹ יַחְדָּו׃

Gadlu Ladonai itti, u-n'romemah sh'mo yachdav
Make the Lord great with me, and together let us exalt Its name.
    PSALM 34:4

אוֹר זָרֻעַ לַצַּדִּיק וּלְיִשְׁרֵי־לֵב שִׂמְחָה:

Or Zaru'a latzaddik, u-l'yishrei lev simkhah
Light is planted for the righteous and joy for those upright of heart.
PSALM 97:11

הָרִיעוּ לַיהוָה כָּל־הָאָרֶץ פִּצְחוּ וְרַנְּנוּ וְזַמֵּרוּ:

Hari'u Ladonai kol ha'aretz, pitzchu v'ranenu v'zameiru
Shout joyfully to the Lord, all the earth, make a loud noise, rejoice, and sing.
PSALM 98:4

קוֹל־יְהוָה בַּכֹּחַ קוֹל יְהוָה בֶּהָדָר:

Kol Adonai bako'ach, kol Adonai behadar
The voice [essence] of the Lord is within power, the voice [essence] of the Lord is within beauty.
PSALM 29:4

לְמַעַן יֵחָלְצוּן יְדִידֶיךָ הוֹשִׁיעָה יְמִינְךָ וַעֲנֵנִי:

La'ma'an yeichaltzoon y'didekha, hoshi'ah yeminkha va'aneini!
That you may deliver your loved ones, save with your right hand [the hand of lovingkindness], and answer me.
PSALM 60:7

יִהְיוּ לְרָצוֹן | אִמְרֵי־פִי וְהֶגְיוֹן לִבִּי לְפָנֶיךָ יְהוָה צוּרִי וְגֹאֲלִי:

Yihiyu l'ratzon imrei fi v'hegyon libi l'fanekha, Adonei tzuri v'go'ali
May the words of my mouth and the meditations of my heart be acceptable before you, Lord, my rock and redeemer.
PSALM 19:15

הַשָּׁמַיִם שָׁמַיִם לַיהֹוָה וְהָאָרֶץ נָתַן לִבְנֵי־אָדָם:

Hashamayim shamayim Ladonai, v'ha'aretz natan livnei adam
Heaven belongs to the Lord, and It gave the earth to humankind.
    PSALM 115:16

הָרוֹפֵא לִשְׁבוּרֵי לֵב וּמְחַבֵּשׁ לְעַצְּבוֹתָם:

Ha-rofei lishvurei lev, u-mechabeish l'atzvotam
The healer of the brokenhearted will bind up their wounds.
    PSALM 147:3

אָהַבְתִּי כִּי־יִשְׁמַע יְהֹוָה אֶת־קוֹלִי תַּחֲנוּנָי:

Ahavti ki yishma Adonai et koli tachanunai
I love that the Lord will hear my voice and my prayers.
    PSALM 116:1

אָנָּה יְהֹוָה מַלְּטָה נַפְשִׁי:

Ana Adonai maltah nafshi
Please, Lord, deliver my soul.
    PSALM 116:4

יְהֹוָה לִי לֹא אִירָא:

Adonai li lo ira
The Lord is with me, I shall not fear.
    PSALM 118:6

יְהֹוָה עֹז לְעַמּוֹ יִתֵּן יְהֹוָה יְבָרֵךְ אֶת־עַמּוֹ בַשָּׁלוֹם:

Adonai oz l'amo yittein, Adonai yevareikh et ammo vashalom
The Lord gives power to Its people, the Lord blesses Its people with peace.
    PSALM 29:11

Appendix 2

Schedules for One-Day Retreats

Schedule for One-Day Retreat to Heal Relationships

Sitting Practice ....45 minutes
Meditative Prayer ....60–90 minutes
Tehora He/Pure Soul Meditation ....45 minutes
Chesed: The Lovingkindness Meditation ....45 minutes
Walking Meditation...45 minutes
Meditative Eating ....60 minutes
Rest
Reflections on the Psalms ....45 minutes
Kabbalistic Dream-Healing ....45 minutes
Hitbodedut: Alone with God ....45 minutes
Kavannah and Continuity Practice.....................45 minutes
Raising Holy Sparks ....45 minutes
Sitting Practice ....45 minutes

Schedule for One-Day Physical/Spiritual Retreat

Ablutions/*Mikveh* ....60 minutes
Sitting Practice ....45 minutes
Morning Blessings ....45 minutes
Yihudim Chanting Meditation...........................45 minutes
Meditative Eating ....60 minutes
Rest
Sitting Practice ....45 minutes
Four Worlds ....45 minutes
Walking Meditation...45 minutes
Inner Harmony..45 minutes
Psycho-Spiritual Journaling................................60 minutes

Schedule for One-Day Emotional/Spiritual Retreat

Sitting Practice ....45 minutes
Lucid Strolling ....45 minutes
Meditative Prayer...60 minutes
Divine Protection...45 minutes
Tehora He/Pure Soul Meditation ....45 minutes
Meditative Eating...60 minutes
Rest
Reflections on the Psalms.................................45 minutes
Kabbalistic Dream-Healing ....45 minutes
Hishtavut/Equanimity ....45 minutes
Hitbodedut: Alone with God..............................45 minutes
Chesed: The Lovingkindness Meditation ....45 minutes
Psycho-Spiritual Journaling...............................60 minutes

Schedule for One-Day Mental/Imaginal/Spiritual Retreat

Sitting Practice ....45 minutes
Reflections on the Psalms.................................45 minutes
Contemplative Study..60 minutes
Divine Protection...45 minutes
Shadow of God ....45 minutes
Meditative Eating...60 minutes
Rest
Kavannah and Continuity Practice.....................45 minutes
Yihudim Chanting Meditation...........................45 minutes
Four Worlds ....45 minutes
Bittul Ha-Yesh: Meditation on *Ayin*...................45 minutes
Hishtavut/Equanimity ....45 minutes
Psycho-Spiritual Journaling...............................60 minutes

Schedule for One-Day Retreat to Connect with the Divine

Sitting Practice ....45 minutes

Meditative Prayer ....60–90 minutes

Teshuvah: Return of the Soul...............45 minutes

Tehora He/Pure Soul Meditation ....45 minutes

Protection of the Archangels ....30 minutes

Meditative Eating ....60 minutes

Rest

Walking Meditation.............................45 minutes

Hitbodedut: Alone with God ....45 minutes

Bittul Ha-Yesh: Meditation on *Ayin*....45 minutes

Chesed: The Lovingkindness Meditation ....45 minutes

Devekut: Melting into the Devine .....45 minutes

Psycho-Spiritual Journaling.................60 minutes

Schedule for One-Day Heart Opening Retreat

Sitting Practice ....45 minutes

Kabbalistic Dream-Healing ....45 minutes

Tehora He/Pure Soul Meditation ....45 minutes

Chesed: Lovingkindness Meditation ....45 minutes

Lucid Strolling ....30 minutes

Meditative Eating ....60 minutes

Rest

Hitbodedut: Alone with God ....45 minutes

Raising Holy Sparks.............................45 minutes

Divine Protection.................................45 minutes

Tikkun: Healing the Dead...................45 minutes

Devekut: Melting into the Divine ......45 minutes

Protection of the Archangels ....45 minutes

Appendix 3

Ten-Year Calendars

Key

* indicates the following year
# indicates the previous year
+ indicates two chapters read in the same week

Torah Readings for the Book of Genesis

	2001	2002	2003	2004	2005	2006	2007	2008	2009	2010
Bereshit (1:1–5:8)	10/13	10/5	10/25	10/9	10/29	10/21	10/6	10/25	10/17	10/2
Noah (5:9–11:32)	10/20	10/12	11/1	10/16	11/5	10/28	10/13	11/1	10/24	10/9
Lech Lecha (12:1–17:27)	10/27	10/19	11/8	10/23	11/12	11/4	10/20	11/8	10/31	10/16
Vayera (18:1–22:24)	11/3	10/26	11/15	10/30	11/19	11/11	10/27	11/15	11/7	10/23
Hayyei Sarah (23:1–25:18)	11/10	11/2	11/22	11/6	11/26	11/18	11/3	11/22	11/14	10/30
Toledot (25:19–27:9)	11/17	11/9	11/29	11/13	12/3	11/25	11/10	11/29	11/21	11/6
Vayetze (27:10–32:3)	11/24	11/16	12/6	11/20	12/10	12/2	11/17	12/6	11/28	11/13
Vayishlach (32:4–36:43)	12/1	11/23	12/13	11/27	12/17	12/9	11/24	12/13	12/5	11/20
Vayeshev (37:1–40:23)	12/8	11/30	12/20	12/4	12/24	12/16	12/1	12/20	12/12	11/27
Miketz (41:1–44:17)	12/15	12/7	12/27	12/11	12/31	12/23	12/8	12/27	12/19	12/4
Vayigash (44:18–47:27)	12/22	12/14	1/3*	12/18	1/7*	12/30	12/15	1/3*	12/26	12/11
Vayehi (47:28–50:26)	12/29	12/21	1/10*	12/25	1/14*	1/6*	12/22	1/10*	1/2*	12/18

Torah Readings for the Book of Exodus

	2001	2002	2003	2004	2005	2006	2007	2008	2009	2010
Shemot (1:1–6:1)	1/20	1/5	12/28#	1/17	1/1	1/21	1/13	12/29#	1/17	1/9
Va-era (6:2–9:35)	1/27	1/12	1/4	1/24	1/8	1/28	1/20	1/5	1/24	1/16
Bo (10:1–13:16)	2/3	1/19	1/11	1/31	1/15	2/4	1/27	1/12	1/31	1/23
BeShallach (13:17–17:16)	2/10	1/26	1/18	2/7	1/22	2/11	2/3	1/19	2/7	1/30
Yitro (18:1–20:23)	2/17	2/2	1/25	2/14	1/29	2/18	2/10	1/26	2/14	2/6
Mishpatim (21:1–24:18)	2/24	2/9	2/1	2/21	2/5	2/25	2/17	2/2	2/21	2/13
Terumah (25:1–27:21)	3/3	2/16	2/8	2/28	2/12	3/4	2/24	2/9	2/29	2/20
Tetzaveh (28:1–30:10)	3/10	2/23	2/15	3/6	2/19	3/11	3/3	2/16	3/7	2/27
Ki Tissa (30:10–34:35)	3/17	3/2	2/22	3/13	2/26	3/18	3/10	2/23	3/14	3/6
Vayakhel (35:1–38:20)	3/24+	3/9+	3/1	3/20+	3/5	3/25+	3/17+	3/1	3/21+	3/13+
Pekudei (38:21–40:38)	3/24+	3/9+	3/8	3/20+	3/12	3/25+	3/17+	3/8	3/21+	3/13+

Torah Readings for the Book of Leviticus

	2001	2002	2003	2004	2005	2006	2007	2008	2009	2010
Vayikra (1:1–5:26)	3/31	3/16	3/15	3/27	3/19	4/1	3/24	3/15	3/28	3/20
Tzav (6:1–8:36)	4/7	3/23	3/22	4/3	3/26	4/8	3/31	3/22	4/4	3/27
Shemini (9:1–11:47)	4/21	4/6	3/29	4/17	4/2	4/22	4/14	3/29	4/18	4/10
Tazria (12:1–13:59)	4/28+	4/13+	4/5	4/24+	4/9	4/29+	4/21+	4/5	4/25+	4/17+
Metzora (14:1–15:33)	4/28+	4/13+	4/12	4/24+	4/16	4/29+	4/21+	4/12	4/25+	4/17+
Aharei-mot (16:1–18:30)	5/5+	4/20+	4/24	5/1+	4/23	5/6+	4/28+	4/19	5/2+	4/24+
Kedoshim (19:1–20:27)	5/5+	4/20+	5/3	5/1+	5/7	5/6+	4/28+	5/3	5/2+	4/24+
Emor (21:1–24:23)	5/12	4/27	5/10	5/8	5/14	5/13	5/5	5/10	5/9	5/1
BeHar (25:1–26:2)	5/19+	5/4+	5/17	5/15+	5/21	5/20+	5/12+	5/17	5/16+	5/8+
BeChukotai (26:3–27:34)	5/19+	5/4+	5/24	5/15+	5/28	5/20+	5/12+	5/24	5/16+	5/8+

Torah Readings for the Book of Numbers

	2001	2002	2003	2004	2005	2006	2007	2008	2009	2010
BeMidbar (1:1–4:20)	5/26	5/11	5/31	5/22	6/4	5/27	5/19	5/31	5/23	5/15
Naso (4:21–7:89)	6/2	5/25	6/14	5/29	6/11	6/10	5/26	6/7	6/6	5/22
BeHa-alotkha (8:1–12:16)	6/9	6/1	6/21	6/5	6/18	6/17	6/2	6/14	6/13	5/29
Shelach (13:1–15:41)	6/16	6/8	6/28	6/12	6/25	6/24	6/9	6/21	6/20	6/5
Korach (16:1–18:32)	6/23	6/15	7/5	6/19	7/2	7/1	6/16	6/28	6/27	6/12
Hukkat (19:1–22:1)	6/30	6/22+	7/12+	6/26	7/9	7/8+	6/23	7/5	7/4+	6/19
Balak (22:2–24:9)	7/7	6/22+	7/12+	7/3	7/16	7/8+	6/30	7/12	7/4+	6/26
Pinchas (24:10–30:1)	7/14	6/29	7/19	7/10	7/23	7/15	7/7	7/19	7/11	7/3
Mattot (30:2–32:42)	7/21+	7/6+	7/26+	7/17+	7/30	7/22+	7/14+	7/26	7/18+	7/10+
Masei (33:1–36:13)	7/21+	7/6+	7/26+	7/17+	8/6	7/22+	7/14+	8/2	7/18+	7/10+

Torah Readings for the Book of Deuteronomy

	2001	2002	2003	2004	2005	2006	2007	2008	2009	2010
Devarim (1:1–3:22)	7/28	7/13	8/2	7/24	8/13	7/29	7/21	8/9	7/25	7/17
VeEthannan (3:23–7:11)	8/4	7/20	8/9	7/31	8/20	8/5	7/28	8/16	8/1	7/24
Ekev (7:12–11:25)	8/11	7/27	8/16	8/7	8/27	8/12	8/4	8/23	8/8	7/31
Reeh (11:26–16:17)	8/18	8/3	8/23	8/14	9/3	8/19	8/11	8/30	8/15	8/7
Shofetim (16:18–21:9)	8/25	8/10	8/30	8/21	9/10	8/26	8/18	9/6	8/22	8/14
Ki Tetze (21:10–25:19)	9/1	8/17	9/6	8/28	9/17	9/2	8/25	9/13	8/29	8/21
Ki Tavo (26:1–29:8)	9/8	8/24	9/13	9/4	9/24	9/9	9/1	9/20	9/5	8/28
Nitzavim (29:9–30:20)	9/15	8/31+	9/20+	9/11+	10/1	9/16+	9/8+	9/27	9/12+	9/4+
Vayelech (31:1–31:30)	9/22	8/31+	9/20+	9/11+	10/8	9/16+	9/8+	10/4	9/12+	9/4+
Ha-azinu (32:1–32:52)	9/29	9/14	10/4	9/18	10/15	9/30	9/15	10/11	9/26	9/11
Vezot Habrakhah (33:1–34:12)	10/10	9/29	10/19	10/8	10/26	10/15	10/5	10/22	10/11	10/1

Jewish Holy Days

(The day begins at sundown the night before the date given.)

	2001	2002	2003	2004	2005	2006	2007	2008	2009	2010
Tu b'Shevat	2/8	1/28	1/18	2/7	1/25	2/13	2/3	1/22	2/9	1/30
Purim	3/9	2/26	3/18	3/7	3/25	3/14	3/4	3/21	3/10	2/28
Passover	4/8	3/28	4/17	4/6	4/24	4/13	4/3	4/20	4/9	3/30
Shavuot	5/28	5/17	6/6	5/26	6/13	6/2	5/23	6/9	5/29	5/19
Tisha b'Av	7/29	7/18	8/7	7/27	8/14	8/3	7/24	8/10	7/30	7/20
Rosh Hashana	9/18	9/7	9/27	9/16	10/4	9/23	9/13	9/30	9/19	9/9
Yom Kippur	9/27	9/16	10/6	9/25	10/13	10/2	9/22	10/9	9/28	9/18
Sukkot	10/2	9/21	10/11	9/30	10/18	10/7	9/27	10/14	10/3	9/23
Sh'mni Atzeret	10/9	9/28	10/18	10/7	10/25	10/14	10/4	10/21	10/10	9/30
Chanukkah	12/10	11/30	12/20	12/8	12/26	12/16	12/5	12/22	12/12	12/2

Recommended Books and Resources

There are thousands of inspirational books that could be useful for meditation and spiritual retreats. This list focuses on books and tapes that have Jewish content, many of which are little known by the general public. Major cities have bookstores that specialize in Jewish books, and most of the books on this list can be found through websites. All the listed books are in English.

Ben-Amos, D., and J. R. Mintz. *In Praise of the Baal Shem Tov.* New York: Schocken Books, 1970.

Bokser, Ben Zion. *Abraham Isaac Kook.* New York: Paulist Press, 1978.
_____. *The Jewish Mystical Tradition.* New York: Pilgrim Press, 1981.

Buber, Martin. *The Legend of the Baal-Shem.* New York: Schocken Books, 1955.
_____. *Tales of the Hasidim.* 2 vols. New York: Schocken Books, 1947.
_____. *Ten Rungs: Hasidic Sayings.* New York: Schocken Books, 1962.

Buxbaum, Yitzhak. *Jewish Spiritual Practices.* Northvale, N.J.: Jason Aronson, 1990.

Cooper, David A. *Three Gates to Meditation Practice: A Personal Journey into Sufism, Buddhism, and Judaism.* Woodstock, Vt.: SkyLight Paths, 2000.
_____. *God Is a Verb: Kabbalah and the Practice of Mystical Judaism.* New York: Riverhead, 1997.
_____. *A Heart of Stillness: A Complete Guide to Learning the Art of Meditation.* Woodstock, Vt.: SkyLight Paths, 1999.
_____. *Silence, Simplicity & Solitude: A Complete Guide to Spiritual Retreat at Home.* Woodstock, Vt.: SkyLight Paths, 1999.
_____. *The Mystical Kabbalah.* Boulder, Colo.: Sounds True Audio, 1994. Audiotapes.
_____. *Kabbalah Meditation.* Boulder, Colo.: Sounds True Audio, 1995. Audiotapes.
_____. *The Holy Chariot.* Boulder, Colo.: Sounds True Audio, 1998. Audiotapes.

Cordovero, Rabbi Moses. *The Palm Tree of Deborah.* Translated by Louis Jacobs. New York: Sepher-Hermon Press, 1974.

Davis, Avram. *Meditation from the Heart of Judaism: Today's Teachers Share Their Practices, Techniques, and Faith.* Woodstock, Vt.: Jewish Lights, 1997.
_____. *The Way of Flame: A Guide to the Forgotten Mystical Tradition of Jewish Meditation.* Woodstock, Vt.: Jewish Lights, 1999.

Dosick, Wayne. *Soul Judaism: Dancing with God into a New Era.* Woodstock, Vt.: Jewish Lights, 1999.

Dresner, Samuel H. *The World of a Hasidic Master: Levi Yitzhak of Berditchev.* New York: Shapolsky, 1974.

Ginzberg, Louis. *The Legends of the Jews.* 7 vols. Philadelphia: Jewish Publication Society of America, 1982.

Gefen, Nan Fink. *Discovering Jewish Meditation: Instruction & Guidance for Learning an Ancient Spiritual Practice.* Woodstock, Vt.: Jewish Lights, 1999.

Heschel, Abraham Joshua. *The Earth Is the Lord's.* Woodstock, Vt.: Jewish Lights, 1995.
_____. *Man Is Not Alone.* New York: Farrar, Straus & Giroux, 1979.
_____. *The Prophets.* 2 vols. New York: Harper & Row, 1962.
_____. *The Sabbath.* New York: Farrar, Straus & Giroux, 1951.

Idel, Moshe. *The Mystical Experience in Abraham Abulafia.* New York: SUNY, 1988.
_____. *Studies in Ecstatic Kabbalah.* New York: SUNY, 1988.

Jacobs, Louis. *Hasidic Prayer.* New York: Schocken Books, 1972.
_____. *Hasidic Thought.* New York: Schocken Books, 1976.
_____. *Jewish Mystical Testimonies.* Jerusalem: Keter, 1976.

Jerusalem Bible, The. Jerusalem: Koren, 1984.

Kaplan, Aryeh. *The Bahir.* New York: Samuel Weiser, 1979.
_____. *Chasidic Masters.* New York: Moznaim, 1984.
_____. *Inner Space: Introduction to Kabbalah, Meditation, and Prophesy.* Edited by Abraham Sutton. Jerusalem: Moznaim, 1990.
_____. *Jewish Meditation.* New York: Schocken Books, 1985.
_____. *Meditation and Kabbalah.* York Beach, Maine: Samuel Weiser, 1986.
_____. *Meditation and the Bible.* York Beach, Maine: Samuel Weiser, 1981.
_____. *Sefer Yetzirah: The Book of Creation.* York Beach, Maine: Samuel Weiser, 1990.

Kushner, Lawrence. *The River of Light: Jewish Mystical Awareness.* Woodstock, Vt.: Jewish Lights, 2000.
_____. *Honey from the Rock: An Introduction to Jewish Mysticism.* Woodstock, Vt.: Jewish Lights, 1997.

Langer, Jiri. *Nine Gates to the Chassidic Mysteries.* New York: Behrman House, 1976.

Levin, Meyer. *Classic Hassidic Tales.* New York: Viking Penguin, 1975.

Mintz, Jerome R. *Legends of the Hasidim.* Chicago: University of Chicago Press, 1968.

Schachter, Rabbi Zalman. *Fragments of a Future Scroll.* Germantown, Pa.: Leaves of Grass Press, 1975.
_____. *Paradigm Shift.* Northvale, N.J.: Jason Aronson, 1993.
_____, with Donald Gropman. *The First Step: A Guide for the New Jewish Spirit.* New York: Bantam Books, 1983.

Schneider, Susie. *A Still Small Voice: Correspondence Teachings in Classic Jewish Wisdom.* Excellent privately published monographs in Israel on Kabbalah. P.O. Box 14503, Jerusalem, Israel, 91141.

Scholem, Gershom. *Major Trends in Jewish Mysticism.* New York: Schocken Books, 1946.

Shapiro, Rami M. *Wisdom of the Jewish Sages.* New York: Bell Tower, 1995.

Steinsaltz, Rabbi Adm. *Beggars and Prayers.* New York: Basic Books, 1979.
_____. *The Sustaining Utterance: Discourses on Chasidic Thought.* Northvale, N.J.: Jason Aronson, 1989.
_____. *The Thirteen Petalled Rose.* New York: Basic Books, 1980.

Waskow, Arthur. *God-Wrestling.* New York: Schocken Books, 1978.
_____. *Seasons of Our Joy.* New York: Bantam Books, 1982; Boston: Beacon Press, 1991.

Weiner, Herbert. *Nine and a Half Mystics: The Kabbalah Today.* New York: Macmillan, Collier Books, 1969.

Wiesel, Elie. *Legends of Our Time.* New York: Schocken Books, 1982.
_____. *Somewhere a Master.* New York: Simon & Schuster, Summit Books, 1982.
_____. *Souls on Fire.* New York: Random House, 1972.

Winkler, Gershon. *The Golem of Prague.* New York: Judaica Press, 1980.
_____. *They Called Her Rebbe: The Maiden of Ludomir.* New York: Judaica Press, 1991.

The follow organizations have a wide variety of diverse programs including classes, workshops, and retreats in Jewish meditation, Kabbalah, Hasidism, and other subjects of general interest in the Jewish world. Many of their websites have links to other organizations, and are kept current in these rapidly changing times.

Aleph, Alliance for Jewish Renewal, 7318 Germantown Ave., Philadelphia, PA 19119-1793; www.aleph.org

Elat Chayyim, a Center for Healing and Renewal, 99 Mill Hook Rd., Accord, NY 12404; (800) 398-2630, www.elatchayyim.com

Chochmat HaLev, 2215 Prince St., Berkeley, CA 94705; (510) 704-9687; www.chochmat.com

Metivta, a Center for Contemplative Judaism, 2001 South Barrington #106, Los Angeles, CA 90025-5363; (310) 477-5370; www.metivta.org

National Havurah Committee, 7318 Germantown Ave., Philadelphia, PA 19119-1720; (215) 247-9703.

About JEWISH LIGHTS Publishing

People of all faiths and backgrounds yearn for books that attract, engage, educate and spiritually inspire.

Our principal goal is to stimulate thought and help all people learn about who the Jewish People are, where they come from, and what the future can be made to hold. While people of our diverse Jewish heritage are the primary audience, our books speak to people in the Christian world as well and will broaden their understanding of Judaism and the roots of their own faith.

We bring to you authors who are at the forefront of spiritual thought and experience. While each has something different to say, they all say it in a voice that you can hear.

Our books are designed to welcome you and then to engage, stimulate and inspire. We judge our success not only by whether or not our books are beautiful and commercially successful, but by whether or not they make a difference in your life.

We at Jewish Lights take great care to produce beautiful books that present meaningful spiritual content in a form that reflects the art of making high quality books. Therefore, we want to acknowledge those who contributed to the production of this book.

Stuart M. Matlins, Publisher

PRODUCTION
Marian B. Wallace & Bridgett Taylor

EDITORIAL
Sandra Korinchak, Emily Wichland,
Martha McKinney & Amanda Dupuis

COVER DESIGN
Graciela Galup, Graciela Galup Book Design,
Cambridge, Massachusetts

TYPESETTING
Doug Porter, Desktop Services & Publishing,
San Antonio, Texas

COVER & TEXT PRINTING AND BINDING
Versa Press, East Peoria, Illinois

Meditation Audiotapes
by Rabbi David A. Cooper

The Holy Chariot
Twelve meditative practices that lead to a higher state of consciousness.
6 tapes, 9 hrs. ISBN 1-56455-584-4 $59.95

Kabbalah Meditation
Includes most of the meditations found in the Kabbalah section of *The Handbook of Jewish Meditation Practices: A Guide for Enriching the Sabbath and Other Days of Your Life.* 2 tapes, 2 hrs. ISBN 1-56455-335-3 $17.95

The Mystical Kabbalah
Contains the meditations of *Kabbalah Meditation* (see above), plus more information on the basics of Kabbalah. 5 tapes, 7 hrs. ISBN 1-56455-289-6 $49.95

_____ copies of *The Holy Chariot* @ $59.95 each = $ _____

_____ copies of *Kabbalah Meditation* @ $17.95 each = $ _____

_____ copies of *The Mystical Kabbalah* @ $49.95 each = $ _____

Add s/h* = $ _____

TOTAL = $ _____

Prices subject to change

❏ Check enclosed for $ _____ payable to: **JEWISH LIGHTS PUBLISHING**

Credit Card: ❏ VISA   ❏ MasterCard

Name on Card _____

Cardholder Address: Street _____

City/State/Zip _____ Phone (____)_____

Credit Card # _____ Exp. Date _____

Signature _____

Please send to: ❏ Same as Above ❏ Address Below

Name _____

Street _____

City/State/Zip _____ Phone (____)_____

* Shipping/handling within U.S./Canada: $3.50 for first tape set and $2.00 each add'l set to a maximum of $15.00; Outside U.S./Canada: $9.00 for first tape set and $3.00 ea. add'l set via surface mail insured.

JEWISH LIGHTS Publishing
Sunset Farm Offices, Rte. 4, P.O. Box 237
Woodstock, Vermont 05091
Tel: (802) 457-4000   Fax: (802) 457-4004
www.jewishlights.com

Credit Card Orders: 800-962-4544 (9 AM–5 PM ET, M–F)

Spirituality

The Women's Torah Commentary: *New Insights from Women Rabbis on the 54 Weekly Torah Portions* Ed. by *Rabbi Elyse Goldstein*

For the first time, women rabbis provide a commentary on the entire Torah. More than 25 years after the first woman was ordained a rabbi in America, women have an impressive group of spiritual role models that they never had before. Here, in a week-by-week format, these inspiring teachers bring their rich perspectives to bear on the biblical text. A perfect gift for others, or for yourself. 6 x 9, 496 pp, HC, ISBN 1-58023-076-8 **$34.95**

Bringing the Psalms to Life
How to Understand and Use the Book of Psalms by *Rabbi Daniel F. Polish*

Here, the most beloved—and least understood—of the books in the Bible comes alive. This simultaneously insightful and practical guide shows how the psalms address a myriad of spiritual issues in our lives: feeling abandoned, overcoming illness, dealing with anger, and more. 6 x 9, 208 pp, HC, ISBN 1-58023-077-6 **$21.95**

Stepping Stones to Jewish Spiritual Living: *Walking the Path Morning, Noon, and Night* by *Rabbi James L. Mirel* & *Karen Bonnell Werth*

Transforms our daily routine into sacred acts of mindfulness. Chapters are arranged according to the cycle of each day. "A wonderful, practical, and inspiring guidebook to gently bring the riches of Jewish practice into our busy, everyday lives. Highly recommended." —*Rabbi David A. Cooper.* 6 x 9, 240 pp, Quality PB, ISBN 1-58023-074-1 **$16.95**; HC, ISBN 1-58023-003-2 **$21.95**

Parenting As a Spiritual Journey:
Deepening Ordinary & Extraordinary Events into Sacred Occasions
by Rabbi Nancy Fuchs-Kreimer 6 x 9, 224 pp, Quality PB, ISBN 1-58023-016-4 **$16.95**

The Year Mom Got Religion: *One Woman's Midlife Journey into Judaism*
by Lee Meyerhoff Hendler 6 x 9, 208 pp, Quality PB, ISBN 1-58023-070-9 **$15.95**;
HC, ISBN 1-58023-000-8 **$19.95**

Moses—The Prince, the Prophet: *His Life, Legend & Message for Our Lives*
by Rabbi Levi Meier, Ph.D. 6 x 9, 224 pp, Quality PB, ISBN 1-58023-069-5 **$16.95**;
HC, ISBN 1-58023-013-X **$23.95**

Ancient Secrets: *Using the Stories of the Bible to Improve Our Everyday Lives*
by Rabbi Levi Meier, Ph.D. 5½ x 8½, 288 pp, Quality PB, ISBN 1-58023-064-4 **$16.95**

Spirituality—The Kushner Series

Honey from the Rock, Special Anniversary Edition
An Introduction to Jewish Mysticism
by *Lawrence Kushner*

An insightful and absorbing introduction to the ten gates of Jewish mysticism and how it applies to daily life. "The easiest introduction to Jewish mysticism you can read."
6 x 9, 176 pp, Quality PB, ISBN 1-58023-073-3 **$15.95**

Eyes Remade for Wonder
The Way of Jewish Mysticism and Sacred Living
A Lawrence Kushner Reader

Intro. by *Thomas Moore*

Whether you are new to Kushner or a devoted fan, you'll find inspiration here. With samplings from each of Kushner's works, and a generous amount of new material, this book is to be read and reread, each time discovering deeper layers of meaning in our lives.
6 x 9, 240 pp, Quality PB, ISBN 1-58023-042-3 **$16.95**; HC, ISBN 1-58023-014-8 **$23.95**

Invisible Lines of Connection
Sacred Stories of the Ordinary
by *Lawrence Kushner* AWARD WINNER!

Through his everyday encounters with family, friends, colleagues and strangers, Kushner takes us deeply into our lives, finding flashes of spiritual insight in the process.
6 x 9, 160 pp, Quality PB, ISBN 1-879045-98-2 **$15.95**; HC, ISBN 1-879045-52-4 **$21.95**

 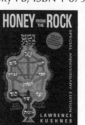   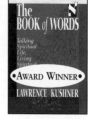

The Book of Letters
A Mystical Hebrew Alphabet AWARD WINNER!
by Lawrence Kushner
Popular HC Edition, 6 x 9, 80 pp, 2-color text, ISBN 1-879045-00-1 **$24.95**; *Deluxe Gift Edition,* 9 x 12, 80 pp, HC, 2-color text, ornamentation, slipcase, ISBN 1-879045-01-X **$79.95**; *Collector's Limited Edition,* 9 x 12, 80 pp, HC, gold-embossed pages, hand-assembled slipcase. With silkscreened print. Limited to 500 signed and numbered copies, ISBN 1-879045-04-4 **$349.00**

The Book of Words
Talking Spiritual Life, Living Spiritual Talk AWARD WINNER!
by Lawrence Kushner 6 x 9, 160 pp, Quality PB, 2-color text, ISBN 1-58023-020-2 **$16.95**; 152 pp, HC, ISBN 1-879045-35-4 **$21.95**

God Was in This Place & I, i Did Not Know
Finding Self, Spirituality & Ultimate Meaning
by Lawrence Kushner 6 x 9, 192 pp, Quality PB, ISBN 1-879045-33-8 **$16.95**

The River of Light: *Jewish Mystical Awareness*
by Lawrence Kushner 6 x 9, 192 pp, Quality PB, ISBN 1-879045-03-6 **$14.95**

Spirituality

My People's Prayer Book: *Traditional Prayers, Modern Commentaries*

Ed. by *Dr. Lawrence A. Hoffman*

This momentous, critically-acclaimed series is truly a people's prayer book, one that provides a diverse and exciting commentary to the traditional liturgy. It will help modern men and women find new wisdom and guidance in Jewish prayer, and bring liturgy into their lives. Each book includes Hebrew text, modern translation, and commentaries *from all perspectives* of the Jewish world. Vol. 1—*The Sh'ma and Its Blessings,* 7 x 10, 168 pp, HC, ISBN 1-879045-79-6 **$23.95**
Vol. 2—*The Amidah,* 7 x 10, 240 pp, HC, ISBN 1-879045-80-X **$23.95**
Vol. 3—*P'sukei D'zimrah* (Morning Psalms), 7 x 10, 240 pp, HC, ISBN 1-879045-81-8 **$23.95**
Vol. 4—*Seder K'riyat Hatorah* (Shabbat Torah Service), 7 x 10, 240 pp, ISBN 1-879045-82-6 **$23.95**

Voices from Genesis: *Guiding Us through the Stages of Life*

by *Dr. Norman J. Cohen*

In a brilliant blending of modern *midrash* (finding contemporary meaning from biblical texts) and the life stages of Erik Erikson's developmental psychology, the characters of Genesis come alive to give us insights for our own journeys. 6 x 9, 192 pp, HC, ISBN 1-879045-75-3 **$21.95**

God Whispers: *Stories of the Soul, Lessons of the Heart*
by Rabbi Karyn D. Kedar 6 x 9, 176 pp, Quality PB, ISBN 1-58023-088-1 **$15.95**;
HC, ISBN 1-58023-023-7 **$19.95**

Being God's Partner: *How to Find the Hidden Link Between Spirituality and Your Work*
by Rabbi Jeffrey K. Salkin; Intro. by Norman Lear AWARD WINNER!
6 x 9, 192 pp, Quality PB, ISBN 1-879045-65-6 **$16.95**; HC, ISBN 1-879045-37-0 **$19.95**

ReVisions: *Seeing Torah through a Feminist Lens* AWARD WINNER!
by Rabbi Elyse Goldstein 5½ x 8½, 208 pp, HC, ISBN 1-58023-047-4 **$19.95**

Soul Judaism: *Dancing with God into a New Era*
by Rabbi Wayne Dosick 5½ x 8½, 304 pp, Quality PB, ISBN 1-58023-053-9 **$16.95**

Finding Joy: *A Practical Spiritual Guide to Happiness* AWARD WINNER!
by Rabbi Dannel I. Schwartz with Mark Hass
6 x 9, 192 pp, Quality PB, ISBN 1-58023-009-1 **$14.95**; HC, ISBN 1-879045-53-2 **$19.95**

The Empty Chair: *Finding Hope and Joy—*
Timeless Wisdom from a Hasidic Master, Rebbe Nachman of Breslov AWARD WINNER!
Adapted by Moshe Mykoff and the Breslov Research Institute
4 x 6, 128 pp, Deluxe PB, 2-color text, ISBN 1-879045-67-2 **$9.95**

The Gentle Weapon: *Prayers for Everyday and Not-So-Everyday Moments*
Adapted from the Wisdom of Rebbe Nachman of Breslov by Moshe Mykoff and
S. C. Mizrahi, with the Breslov Research Institute
4 x 6, 144 pp, Deluxe PB, 2-color text, ISBN 1-58023-022-9 **$9.95**

"Who Is a Jew?" *Conversations, Not Conclusions* by Meryl Hyman
6 x 9, 272 pp, Quality PB, ISBN 1-58023-052-0 **$16.95**; HC, ISBN 1-879045-76-1 **$23.95**

Spirituality & More

These Are the Words: *A Vocabulary of Jewish Spiritual Life*

by *Arthur Green*

What are the most essential ideas, concepts and terms that an educated person needs to know about Judaism? From *Adonai* (My Lord) to *zekhut* (merit), this enlightening and entertaining journey through Judaism teaches us the 149 core Hebrew words that constitute the basic vocabulary of Jewish spiritual life. 6 x 9, 304 pp, HC, ISBN 1-58023-024-5 **$21.95**

The Enneagram and Kabbalah: *Reading Your Soul*

by *Rabbi Howard A. Addison*

Combines two of the most powerful maps of consciousness known to humanity—The Tree of Life (the *Sefirot*) from the Jewish mystical tradition of *Kabbalah*, and the nine-pointed Enneagram—and shows how, together, they can provide a powerful tool for self-knowledge, critique, and transformation. 6 x 9, 176 pp, Quality PB, ISBN 1-58023-001-6 **$15.95**

Embracing the Covenant
Converts to Judaism Talk About Why & How

Ed. and with Intros. by *Rabbi Allan L. Berkowitz* and *Patti Moskovitz*

Through personal experiences of 20 converts to Judaism, this book illuminates reasons for converting, the quest for a satisfying spirituality, the appeal of the Jewish tradition and how conversion has changed lives—the convert's, and the lives of those close to them. 6 x 9, 192 pp, Quality PB, ISBN 1-879045-50-8 **$15.95**

Shared Dreams: *Martin Luther King, Jr. and the Jewish Community*
by Rabbi Marc Schneier; Preface by Martin Luther King III
6 x 9, 240 pp, HC, ISBN 1-58023-062-8 **$24.95**

Mystery Midrash: *An Anthology of Jewish Mystery & Detective Fiction*
Ed. by Lawrence W. Raphael; Preface by Joel Siegel, ABC's *Good Morning America*
6 x 9, 304 pp, Quality PB, ISBN 1-58023-055-5 **$16.95**

The Jewish Gardening Cookbook: *Growing Plants & Cooking for Holidays & Festivals*
by Michael Brown 6 x 9, 224 pp, HC, Illus., ISBN 1-58023-004-0 **$21.95**

Wandering Stars: *An Anthology of Jewish Fantasy & Science Fiction* Ed. by Jack Dann; Intro. by Isaac Asimov 6 x 9, 272 pp, Quality PB, ISBN 1-58023-005-9 **$16.95**

More Wandering Stars
An Anthology of Outstanding Stories of Jewish Fantasy and Science Fiction
Ed. by Jack Dann; Intro. by Isaac Asimov 6 x 9, 192 pp, Quality PB, ISBN 1-58023-063-6 **$16.95**

A Heart of Wisdom: *Making the Jewish Journey from Midlife through the Elder Years*
Ed. by Susan Berrin; Foreword by Harold Kushner
6 x 9, 384 pp, Quality PB, ISBN 1-58023-051-2 **$18.95**; HC, ISBN 1-879045-73-7 **$24.95**

Sacred Intentions: *Daily Inspiration to Strengthen the Spirit, Based on Jewish Wisdom*
by Rabbi Kerry M. Olitzky and Rabbi Lori Forman
4½ x 6½, 448 pp, Quality PB, ISBN 1-58023-061-X **$15.95**

Healing/Wellness/Recovery

Jewish Pastoral Care
A Practical Handbook from Traditional and Contemporary Sources
Ed. by *Rabbi Dayle A. Friedman*

This innovative resource builds on the classic foundations of pastoral care, enriching it with uniquely Jewish traditions and wisdom. Gives today's Jewish pastoral counselors practical guidelines based in the Jewish tradition. 6 x 9, 352 pp, HC, ISBN 1-58023-078-4 **$34.95** (Avail. Jan. 2001)

Healing of Soul, Healing of Body
Spiritual Leaders Unfold the Strength & Solace in Psalms
Ed. by *Rabbi Simkha Y. Weintraub, CSW*, for The National Center for Jewish Healing

A source of solace for those who are facing illness, as well as those who care for them. Provides a wellspring of strength with inspiring introductions and commentaries by eminent spiritual leaders reflecting all Jewish movements. 6 x 9, 128 pp, Quality PB, Illus., 2-color text, ISBN 1-879045-31-1 **$14.95**

Self, Struggle & Change: *Family Conflict Stories in Genesis and Their Healing Insights for Our Lives*
by *Dr. Norman J. Cohen*

How do I find wholeness in my life and in my family's life? Here a modern master of biblical interpretation brings us greater understanding of the ancient text and of ourselves in this intriguing re-telling of conflict between husband and wife, father and son, brothers and sisters. 6 x 9, 224 pp, Quality PB, ISBN 1-879045-66-4 **$16.95**; HC, ISBN 1-879045-19-2 **$21.95**

Twelve Jewish Steps to Recovery: *A Personal Guide to Turning from Alcoholism & Other Addictions . . . Drugs, Food, Gambling, Sex . . .* by Rabbi Kerry M. Olitzky & Stuart A. Copans, M.D. Preface by Abraham J. Twerski, M.D.; Intro. by Rabbi Sheldon Zimmerman; "Getting Help"by JACS Foundation 6 x 9, 144 pp, Quality PB, ISBN 1-879045-09-5 **$13.95**

One Hundred Blessings Every Day: *Daily Twelve Step Recovery Affirmations, Exercises for Personal Growth & Renewal Reflecting Seasons of the Jewish Year* by Rabbi Kerry M. Olitzky, with selected meditations prepared by Rabbi James Stone Goodman, Danny Siegel, and Gordon Tucker. Foreword by Rabbi Neil Gillman, The Jewish Theological Seminary of America; Afterword by Dr. Jay Holder, Director, Exodus Treatment Center 4½ x 6½, 432 pp, Quality PB, ISBN 1-879045-30-3 **$14.95**

Recovery from Codependence: *A Jewish Twelve Steps Guide to Healing Your Soul* by Rabbi Kerry M. Olitzky; Foreword by Marc Galanter, M.D., Director, Division of Alcoholism & Drug Abuse, NYU Medical Center; Afterword by Harriet Rossetto, Director, Gateways Beit T'shuvah 6 x 9, 160 pp, Quality PB, ISBN 1-879045-32-X **$13.95**; HC, ISBN 1-879045-27-3 **$21.95**

Renewed Each Day: *Daily Twelve Step Recovery Meditations Based on the Bible* by Rabbi Kerry M. Olitzky & Aaron Z. *Vol. I: Genesis & Exodus*; Intro. by Rabbi Michael A. Signer; Afterword by JACS Foundation. *Vol. II: Leviticus, Numbers and Deuteronomy*; Intro. by Sharon M. Strassfeld; Afterword by Rabbi Harold M. Schulweis
Vol. I: 6 x 9, 224 pp, Quality PB, ISBN 1-879045-12-5 **$14.95**
Vol. II: 6 x 9, 280 pp, Quality PB, ISBN 1-879045-13-3 **$14.95**

Life Cycle & Holidays

How to Be a Perfect Stranger, In 2 Volumes
A Guide to Etiquette in Other People's Religious Ceremonies
Ed. by *Stuart M. Matlins* & *Arthur J. Magida* AWARD WINNER!

What will happen? What do I do? What do I wear? What do I say? What should I avoid doing, wearing, saying? What are their basic beliefs? Should I bring a gift? In question-and-answer format, *How to Be a Perfect Stranger* explains the rituals and celebrations of America's major religions/denominations, helping an interested guest to feel comfortable, participate to the fullest extent possible, and avoid violating anyone's religious principles. It is not a guide to theology, nor is it presented from the perspective of any particular faith.
Vol. 1: *America's Largest Faiths,* 6 x 9, 432 pp, HC, ISBN 1-879045-39-7 **$24.95**
Vol. 2: *Other Faiths in America,* 6 x 9, 416 pp, HC, ISBN 1-879045-63-X **$24.95**

Putting God on the Guest List, 2nd Ed.
How to Reclaim the Spiritual Meaning of Your Child's Bar or Bat Mitzvah
by *Rabbi Jeffrey K. Salkin* AWARD WINNER!

The expanded, updated, revised edition of today's most influential book (over 60,000 copies in print) about finding core spiritual values in American Jewry's most misunderstood ceremony.
6 x 9, 224 pp, Quality PB, ISBN 1-879045-59-1 **$16.95**; HC, ISBN 1-879045-58-3 **$24.95**

For Kids—Putting God on Your Guest List
How to Claim the Spiritual Meaning of Your Bar or Bat Mitzvah
by Rabbi Jeffrey K. Salkin 6 x 9, 144 pp, Quality PB, ISBN 1-58023-015-6 **$14.95**

Bar/Bat Mitzvah Basics
A Practical Family Guide to Coming of Age Together
Ed. by Cantor Helen Leneman 6 x 9, 240 pp, Quality PB, ISBN 1-879045-54-0 **$16.95**; HC, ISBN 1-879045-51-6 **$24.95**

The New Jewish Baby Book AWARD WINNER!
Names, Ceremonies, & Customs—A Guide for Today's Families
by Anita Diamant 6 x 9, 336 pp, Quality PB, ISBN 1-879045-28-1 **$16.95**

Hanukkah: The Art of Jewish Living
by Dr. Ron Wolfson 7 x 9, 192 pp, Quality PB, Illus., ISBN 1-879045-97-4 **$16.95**

The Shabbat Seder: The Art of Jewish Living
by Dr. Ron Wolfson 7 x 9, 272 pp, Quality PB, Illus., ISBN 1-879045-90-7 **$16.95**
Also available are these helpful companions to *The Shabbat Seder*: Booklet of the Blessings and Songs, ISBN 1-879045-91-5 **$5.00**; Audiocassette of the Blessings, DN03 **$6.00**; Teacher's Guide, ISBN 1-879045-92-3 **$4.95**

The Passover Seder: The Art of Jewish Living
by Dr. Ron Wolfson 7 x 9, 352 pp, Quality PB, Illus., ISBN 1-879045-93-1 **$16.95**
Also available are these helpful companions to *The Passover Seder*: Passover Workbook, ISBN 1-879045-94-X **$6.95**; Audiocassette of the Blessings, DN04 **$6.00**; Teacher's Guide, ISBN 1-879045-95-8 **$4.95**

Life Cycle

Jewish Paths toward Healing and Wholeness
A Personal Guide to Dealing with Suffering
by *Rabbi Kerry M. Olitzky*; Foreword by *Debbie Friedman*

"Why me?" Why do we suffer? How can we heal? Grounded in the spiritual traditions of Judaism, this book provides healing rituals, psalms and prayers that help readers initiate a dialogue with God, to guide them along the complicated path of healing and wholeness.
6 x 9, 192 pp, Quality PB, ISBN 1-58023-068-7 **$15.95**

Mourning & Mitzvah: *A Guided Journal for Walking the Mourner's Path through Grief to Healing*
by *Anne Brener, L.C.S.W.*; Foreword by *Rabbi Jack Riemer*; Intro. by *Rabbi William Cutter*

For those who mourn a death, for those who would help them, for those who face a loss of any kind, Brener teaches us the power and strength available to us in the fully experienced mourning process. 7½ x 9, 288 pp, Quality PB, ISBN 1-879045-23-0 **$19.95**

Tears of Sorrow, Seeds of Hope
A Jewish Spiritual Companion for Infertility and Pregnancy Loss
by *Rabbi Nina Beth Cardin*

A spiritual companion that enables us to mourn infertility, a lost pregnancy, or a stillbirth within the prayers, rituals, and meditations of Judaism. By drawing on the texts of tradition, it creates readings and rites of mourning, and through them provides a wellspring of compassion, solace—and hope. 6 x 9, 192 pp, HC, ISBN 1-58023-017-2 **$19.95**

Lifecycles
V. 1: *Jewish Women on Life Passages & Personal Milestones* AWARD WINNER!
Ed. and with Intros. by Rabbi Debra Orenstein
V. 2: *Jewish Women on Biblical Themes in Contemporary Life* AWARD WINNER!
Ed. and with Intros. by Rabbi Debra Orenstein and Rabbi Jane Rachel Litman
V. 1: 6 x 9, 480 pp, Quality PB, ISBN 1-58023-018-0 **$19.95**; HC, ISBN 1-879045-14-1 **$24.95**
V. 2: 6 x 9, 464 pp, Quality PB, ISBN 1-58023-019-9 **$19.95**; HC, ISBN 1-879045-15-X **$24.95**

Grief in Our Seasons: *A Mourner's Kaddish Companion*
by Rabbi Kerry M. Olitzky 4½ x 6½, 448 pp, Quality PB, ISBN 1-879045-55-9 **$15.95**

A Time to Mourn, A Time to Comfort: *A Guide to Jewish Bereavement and Comfort*
by Dr. Ron Wolfson 7 x 9, 336 pp, Quality PB, ISBN 1-879045-96-6 **$16.95**

When a Grandparent Dies
A Kid's Own Remembering Workbook for Dealing with Shiva and the Year Beyond
by Nechama Liss-Levinson, Ph.D.
8 x 10, 48 pp, HC, Illus., 2-color text, ISBN 1-879045-44-3 **$15.95**

So That Your Values Live On: *Ethical Wills & How to Prepare Them*
Ed. by Rabbi Jack Riemer & Professor Nathaniel Stampfer
6 x 9, 272 pp, Quality PB, ISBN 1-879045-34-6 **$17.95**

Theology/Philosophy

A Heart of Many Rooms
Celebrating the Many Voices within Judaism
by *Dr. David Hartman* **AWARD WINNER!**

Named a *Publishers Weekly* "Best Book of the Year." Addresses the spiritual and theological questions that face all Jews and all people today. From the perspective of traditional Judaism, Hartman shows that commitment to both Jewish tradition and to pluralism can create understanding between people of different religious convictions.
6 x 9, 352 pp, HC, ISBN 1-58023-048-2 **$24.95**

A Living Covenant: *The Innovative Spirit in Traditional Judaism*
by *Dr. David Hartman* **AWARD WINNER!**

Winner, National Jewish Book Award. Hartman reveals a Judaism grounded in covenant—a relational framework—informed by the metaphor of marital love rather than that of parent-child dependency. 6 x 9, 368 pp, Quality PB, ISBN 1-58023-011-3 **$18.95**

The Death of Death: *Resurrection and Immortality in Jewish Thought*
by *Dr. Neil Gillman* **AWARD WINNER!**

Does death end life, or is it the passage from one stage of life to another? This National Jewish Book Award Finalist explores the original and compelling argument that Judaism, a religion often thought to pay little attention to the afterlife, not only offers us rich ideas on the subject—but delivers a deathblow to death itself. 6 x 9, 336 pp, Quality PB, ISBN 1-58023-081-4 **$18.95**; HC, ISBN 1-879045-61-3 **$23.95**

Aspects of Rabbinic Theology by Solomon Schechter; New Intro. by Dr. Neil Gillman
6 x 9, 448 pp, Quality PB, ISBN 1-879045-24-9 **$19.95**

The Last Trial: *On the Legends and Lore of the Command to Abraham to Offer Isaac as a Sacrifice* by Shalom Spiegel; New Intro. by Judah Goldin
6 x 9, 208 pp, Quality PB, ISBN 1-879045-29-X **$17.95**

Judaism and Modern Man: *An Interpretation of Jewish Religion* by Will Herberg;
New Intro. by Dr. Neil Gillman 5½ x 8½, 336 pp, Quality PB, ISBN 1-879045-87-7 **$18.95**

Seeking the Path to Life **AWARD WINNER!**
Theological Meditations on God and the Nature of People, Love, Life and Death
by Rabbi Ira F. Stone
6 x 9, 160 pp, Quality PB, ISBN 1-879045-47-8 **$14.95**; HC, ISBN 1-879045-17-6 **$19.95**

The Spirit of Renewal: *Finding Faith after the Holocaust* **AWARD WINNER!**
by Rabbi Edward Feld
6 x 9, 224 pp, Quality PB, ISBN 1-879045-40-0 **$16.95**

Tormented Master: *The Life and Spiritual Quest of Rabbi Nahman of Bratslav*
by Dr. Arthur Green
6 x 9, 416 pp, Quality PB, ISBN 1-879045-11-7 **$18.95**

Your Word Is Fire: *The Hasidic Masters on Contemplative Prayer*
Ed. and Trans. with a New Introduction by Dr. Arthur Green and Dr. Barry W. Holtz
6 x 9, 160 pp, Quality PB, ISBN 1-879045-25-7 **$14.95**

Theology/Philosophy

Torah of the Earth: *Exploring 4,000 Years of Ecology in Jewish Thought*
In 2 Volumes Ed. by *Rabbi Arthur Waskow*

Major new resource offering us an invaluable key to understanding the intersection of ecology and Judaism. Leading scholars provide us with a guided tour of ecological thought from four major Jewish viewpoints. Vol. 1: *Biblical Israel & Rabbinic Judaism*, 6 x 9, 272 pp, Quality PB, ISBN 1-58023-086-5 **$19.95**; Vol. 2: *Zionism & Eco-Judaism*, 6 x 9, 336 pp, Quality PB, ISBN 1-58023-087-3 **$19.95**

Broken Tablets: *Restoring the Ten Commandments and Ourselves*
Ed. by *Rabbi Rachel S. Mikva*; Intro. by *Rabbi Lawrence Kushner*;
Afterword by *Rabbi Arnold Jacob Wolf* **AWARD WINNER!**

Twelve outstanding spiritual leaders each share profound and personal thoughts about these biblical commands and why they have such a special hold on us.
6 x 9, 192 pp, HC, ISBN 1-58023-066-0 **$21.95**

Evolving Halakhah: *A Progressive Approach to Traditional Jewish Law*
by *Rabbi Dr. Moshe Zemer*

Innovative and provocative, this book affirms the system of traditional Jewish law, *halakhah*, as flexible enough to accommodate the changing realities of each generation. It shows that the traditional framework for understanding the Torah's commandments can be the living heart of Jewish life for all Jews. 6 x 9, 480 pp, HC, ISBN 1-58023-002-4 **$40.00**

God & the Big Bang
Discovering Harmony Between Science & Spirituality **AWARD WINNER!**
by Daniel C. Matt
6 x 9, 216 pp, Quality PB, ISBN 1-879045-89-3 **$16.95**; HC, ISBN 1-879045-48-6 **$21.95**

Israel—A Spiritual Travel Guide **AWARD WINNER!**
A Companion for the Modern Jewish Pilgrim
by Rabbi Lawrence A. Hoffman 4¾ x 10, 256 pp, Quality PB, ISBN 1-879045-56-7 **$18.95**

Godwrestling—Round 2: *Ancient Wisdom, Future Paths* **AWARD WINNER!**
by Rabbi Arthur Waskow
6 x 9, 352 pp, Quality PB, ISBN 1-879045-72-9 **$18.95**; HC, ISBN 1-879045-45-1 **$23.95**

Ecology & the Jewish Spirit: *Where Nature & the Sacred Meet* Ed. and with Intros. by Ellen Bernstein 6 x 9, 288 pp, Quality PB, ISBN 1-58023-082-2 **$16.95**;
HC, ISBN 1-879045-88-5 **$23.95**

Israel: *An Echo of Eternity* by Abraham Joshua Heschel; New Intro. by
Dr. Susannah Heschel 5½ x 8, 272 pp, Quality PB, ISBN 1-879045-70-2 **$18.95**

The Earth Is the Lord's: *The Inner World of the Jew in Eastern Europe*
by Abraham Joshua Heschel 5½ x 8, 112 pp, Quality PB, ISBN 1-879045-42-7 **$13.95**

A Passion for Truth: *Despair and Hope in Hasidism* by Abraham Joshua Heschel
5½ x 8, 352 pp, Quality PB, ISBN 1-879045-41-9 **$18.95**

Children's Spirituality

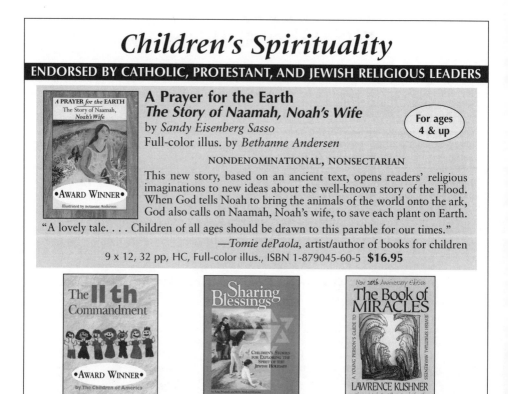

A Prayer for the Earth
The Story of Naamah, Noah's Wife
by *Sandy Eisenberg Sasso*
Full-color illus. by *Bethanne Andersen*

For ages 4 & up

NONDENOMINATIONAL, NONSECTARIAN

This new story, based on an ancient text, opens readers' religious imaginations to new ideas about the well-known story of the Flood. When God tells Noah to bring the animals of the world onto the ark, God also calls on Naamah, Noah's wife, to save each plant on Earth.

"A lovely tale. . . . Children of all ages should be drawn to this parable for our times."
—*Tomie dePaola*, artist/author of books for children

9 x 12, 32 pp, HC, Full-color illus., ISBN 1-879045-60-5 **$16.95**

The 11th Commandment: Wisdom from Our Children
by The Children of America

For all ages

MULTICULTURAL, NONDENOMINATIONAL, NONSECTARIAN

"If there were an Eleventh Commandment, what would it be?" Children of many religious denominations across America answer this question—in their own drawings and words. "A rare book of spiritual celebration for all people, of all ages, for all time."—*Bookviews*
8 x 10, 48 pp, HC, Full-color illus., ISBN 1-879045-46-X **$16.95**

Sharing Blessings: Children's Stories for Exploring the Spirit of the Jewish Holidays
by *Rahel Musleah* and *Rabbi Michael Klayman*
Full-color illus. by *Mary O'Keefe Young*

For ages 6 & up

What is the spiritual message of each of the Jewish holidays? How do we teach it to our children? Many books tell children about the historical significance and customs of the holidays. Now, through engaging, creative stories about one family's preparation, *Sharing Blessings* explores ways to get into the *spirit* of 13 different holidays. "Lighthearted, and yet thorough—allows all Jewish parents (even those with very little Jewish education) to introduce the spirit of our cherished holiday traditions." —*Shari Lewis*, creator and star of PBS' *Lamb Chop's Play-Along*
8½ x 11, 64 pp, HC, Full-color illus., ISBN 1-879045-71-0 **$18.95**

The Book of Miracles
A Young Person's Guide to Jewish Spiritual Awareness
by *Lawrence Kushner*

For ages 9 & up

From the miracle at the Red Sea to the miracle of waking up this morning, this intriguing book introduces kids to a way of everyday spiritual thinking to last a lifetime. Kushner, whose award-winning books have brought spirituality to life for countless adults, now shows young people how to use Judaism as a foundation on which to build their lives. "A well-written, easy to understand, very lovely guide to Jewish spirituality. I recommend it to all teens as a good read." —*Kimberly Kirberger*, co-author, *Chicken Soup for the Teenage Soul* 6 x 9, 96 pp, HC, 2-color illus., ISBN 1-879045-78-8 **$16.95**

Children's Spirituality

God Said Amen
by *Sandy Eisenberg Sasso*
Full-color illus. by *Avi Katz*

For ages 4 & up

MULTICULTURAL, NONDENOMINATIONAL, NONSECTARIAN

A warm and inspiring tale of two kingdoms: Midnight Kingdom is overflowing with water but has no oil to light its lamps; Desert Kingdom is blessed with oil but has no water to grow its gardens. The kingdoms' rulers ask God for help but are too stubborn to ask each other. It takes a minstrel, a pair of royal riding-birds and their young keepers, and a simple act of kindness to show that they need only reach out to each other to find God's answer to their prayers.

9 x 12, 32 pp, HC, Full-color illus., ISBN 1-58023-080-6 **$16.95**

For Heaven's Sake
by *Sandy Eisenberg Sasso*; Full-color illus. by *Kathryn Kunz Finney*

For ages 4 & up

MULTICULTURAL, NONDENOMINATIONAL, NONSECTARIAN

Everyone talked about heaven: "Thank heavens." "Heaven forbid." "For heaven's sake, Isaiah." But no one would say what heaven was or how to find it. So Isaiah decides to find out, by seeking answers from many different people. "This book is a reminder of how well Sandy Sasso knows the minds of children. But it may surprise—and delight—readers to find how well she knows us grown-ups too." —*Maria Harris*, National Consultant in Religious Education, and author of *Teaching and Religious Imagination* 9 x 12, 32 pp, HC, Full-color illus., ISBN 1-58023-054-7 **$16.95**

But God Remembered: Stories of Women from Creation to the Promised Land
by *Sandy Eisenberg Sasso*; Full-color illus. by *Bethanne Andersen*

For ages 8 & up

NONDENOMINATIONAL, NONSECTARIAN

A fascinating collection of four different stories of women only briefly mentioned in biblical tradition and religious texts. Award-winning author Sasso vibrantly brings to life courageous and strong women from ancient tradition; all teach important values through their actions and faith. "Exquisite. . . . A book of beauty, strength and spirituality." —*Association of Bible Teachers* 9 x 12, 32 pp, HC, Full-color illus., ISBN 1-879045-43-5 **$16.95**

God in Between
by *Sandy Eisenberg Sasso*; Full-color illus. by *Sally Sweetland*

For ages 4 & up

MULTICULTURAL, NONDENOMINATIONAL, NONSECTARIAN

If you wanted to find God, where would you look? A magical, mythical tale that teaches that God can be found where we are: within all of us and the relationships between us. "This happy and wondrous book takes our children on a sweet and holy journey into God's presence." —*Rabbi Wayne Dosick, Ph.D.*, author of *Golden Rules* and *Soul Judaism*

9 x 12, 32 pp, HC, Full-color illus., ISBN 1-879045-86-9 **$16.95**

Children's Spirituality

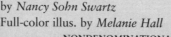

In Our Image
God's First Creatures

For ages
4 & up

by *Nancy Sohn Swartz*

Full-color illus. by *Melanie Hall*

NONDENOMINATIONAL, NONSECTARIAN

A playful new twist on the Creation story—from the perspective of the animals. Celebrates the interconnectedness of nature and the harmony of all living things. "The vibrantly colored illustrations nearly leap off the page in this delightful interpretation." —*School Library Journal*

"A message all children should hear, presented in words and pictures that children will find irresistible." —*Rabbi Harold Kushner,* author of *When Bad Things Happen to Good People*

9 x 12, 32 pp, HC, Full-color illus., ISBN 1-879045-99-0 **$16.95**

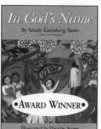

God's Paintbrush

For ages
4 & up

by *Sandy Eisenberg Sasso*; Full-color illus. by *Annette Compton*

MULTICULTURAL, NONDENOMINATIONAL, NONSECTARIAN

Invites children of all faiths and backgrounds to encounter God openly in their own lives. Wonderfully interactive; provides questions adult and child can explore together at the end of each episode. "An excellent way to honor the imaginative breadth and depth of the spiritual life of the young." —*Dr. Robert Coles,* Harvard University

11 x 8½, 32 pp, HC, Full-color illus., ISBN 1-879045-22-2 **$16.95**

Also available: A Teacher's Guide: **A Guide for Jewish & Christian Educators and Parents**
8½ x 11, 32 pp, PB, ISBN 1-879045-57-5 **$6.95**

God's Paintbrush Celebration Kit 9½ x 12, HC, Includes 5 sessions/40 full-color Activity Sheets and Teacher Folder with complete instructions, ISBN 1-58023-050-4 **$21.95**

In God's Name

For ages
4 & up

by *Sandy Eisenberg Sasso*; Full-color illus. by *Phoebe Stone*

MULTICULTURAL, NONDENOMINATIONAL, NONSECTARIAN

Like an ancient myth in its poetic text and vibrant illustrations, this award-winning modern fable about the search for God's name celebrates the diversity and, at the same time, the unity of all the people of the world. "What a lovely, healing book!" —*Madeleine L'Engle*

9 x 12, 32 pp, HC, Full-color illus., ISBN 1-879045-26-5 **$16.95**

What Is God's Name? (A Board Book)

For ages
0–4

An abridged board book version of the award-winning *In God's Name.*

5 x 5, 24 pp, Board, Full-color illus., ISBN 1-893361-10-1 **$7.95**

The Way Into... Series

A major 14-volume series to be completed over the next several years, *The Way Into...* provides an accessible and usable "guided tour" of the Jewish faith, its people, its history and beliefs—in total, an introduction to Judaism for adults that will enable them to understand and interact with sacred texts.

Each volume is written by a major modern scholar and teacher, and is organized around an important concept of Judaism.

The Way Into... will enable all readers to achieve a real sense of Jewish cultural literacy through guided study. Forthcoming volumes include:

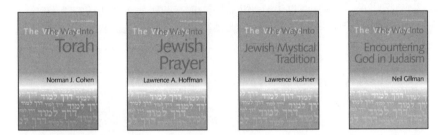

The Way Into Torah

by *Dr. Norman J. Cohen*

What is "Torah"? What are the different approaches to studying Torah? What are the different levels of understanding Torah? For whom is the study intended? Explores the origins and development of Torah, why it should be studied and how to do it. Addresses these and many other issues in this easy-to-use, easy-to-understand introduction to the ancient subject.

6 x 9, 160 pp, HC, ISBN 1-58023-028-8 **$21.95**

The Way Into Jewish Prayer

by *Dr. Lawrence A. Hoffman*

Explores the reasons for and the ways of Jewish prayer. Opens the door to 3,000 years of the Jewish way to God by making available all you need to feel at home in Jewish worship. Provides basic definitions of the terms you need to know as well as thoughtful analysis of the depth that lies beneath Jewish prayer.

6 x 9, 224 pp, HC, ISBN 1-58023-027-X **$21.95**

The Way Into Jewish Mystical Tradition

by *Rabbi Lawrence Kushner*

Explains the principles of Jewish mystical thinking, their religious and spiritual significance, and how they relate to our lives. A book that allows us to experience and understand the Jewish mystical approach to our place in the world.

6 x 9, 176 pp, HC, ISBN 1-58023-029-6 **$21.95** (Avail. Jan. 2001)

The Way Into Encountering God in Judaism

by *Dr. Neil Gillman*

Explains how Jews have encountered God throughout history—and today—by exploring the many metaphors for God in Jewish tradition. Explores the Jewish tradition's passionate but also conflicting ways of relating to God as Creator, relational partner, and a force in history and nature.

6 x 9, 176 pp, HC, ISBN 1-58023-025-3 **$21.95** (Avail. Dec. 2000)

Jewish Meditation

Discovering Jewish Meditation
Instruction & Guidance for Learning an Ancient Spiritual Practice
by *Nan Fink Gefen*

Gives readers of any level of understanding the tools to learn the practice of Jewish meditation on your own, starting you on the path to a deep spiritual and personal connection to God and to greater insight about your life. 6 x 9, 208 pp, Quality PB, ISBN 1-58023-067-9 **$16.95**

Meditation from the Heart of Judaism: *Today's Teachers Share Their Practices, Techniques, and Faith* Ed. by *Avram Davis*
A "how-to"guide for both beginning and experienced meditators, drawing on the wisdom of 22 masters of meditation who explain why and how they meditate. A detailed compendium of the experts' "best practices" offers advice and starting points. 6 x 9, 256 pp, Quality PB, ISBN 1-58023-049-0 **$16.95**; HC, ISBN 1-879045-77-X **$21.95**

The Way of Flame
A Guide to the Forgotten Mystical Tradition of Jewish Meditation
by *Avram Davis* 4½ x 8, 176 pp, Quality PB, ISBN 1-58023-060-1 **$15.95**

Entering the Temple of Dreams: *Jewish Prayers, Movements, and Meditations for the End of the Day* by *Tamar Frankiel* and *Judy Greenfeld*
Nighttime spirituality is much more than bedtime prayers! Here, you'll uncover deeper meaning to familiar nighttime prayers—and learn to combine the prayers with movements and meditations to enhance your physical and psychological well-being.
7 x 10, 192 pp, Quality PB, Illus., ISBN 1-58023-079-2 **$16.95**

Minding the Temple of the Soul: *Balancing Body, Mind, and Spirit through Traditional Jewish Prayer, Movement, and Meditation*
by *Tamar Frankiel* and *Judy Greenfeld*
This new spiritual approach to physical health introduces readers to a spiritual tradition that affirms the body and enables them to reconceive their bodies in a more positive light. Focuses on traditional Jewish prayers, with exercises, movements, and meditations. 7 x 10, 184 pp, Quality PB, Illus., ISBN 1-879045-64-8 **$16.95**; Audiotape of the Blessings, Movements and Meditations (60-min. cassette), JN01 **$9.95**; Videotape of the Movements and Meditations (46-min. VHS), S507 **$20.00**